CLIQUES

ALSO BY CHARLENE C. GIANNETTI
AND MARGARET SAGARESE

The Roller-Coaster Years

Parenting 911

CLIQUES

8 STEPS TO HELP YOUR CHILD SURVIVE THE SOCIAL JUNGLE

Charlene C. Giannetti and Margaret Sagarese

BROADWAY BOOKS

NEW YORK

Broadway Books titles may be purchased for business or promotional use or for special sales. For information, please write to: Special Markets Department, Random House, Inc., 1540 Broadway, New York, NY 10036.

Visit our website at www.broadwaybooks.com

Library of Congress Cataloging-in-Publication Data
Giannetti, Charlene C.
Cliques: 8 steps to help your child survive the social jungle / Charlene C. Giannetti and Margaret Sagarese.
p. cm.
1. Parent and teenager. 2. Middle school students. 3. Peer pressure in adolescence. 4. Cliques (Sociology) I. Title: 8 steps to help your child survive the social jungle. II. Title: Eight steps to help your child survive the social jungle. III. Sagarese, Margaret. IV. Title.
HQ799.15. G53 2001
649'.125—dc21 00-062149

FIRST EDITION

Designed by Cassandra J. Pappas

ISBN 0-7679-0653-5

01 02 03 04 05 10 9 8 7 6 5 4 3 2

For our daughters, Theresa and Skyler Rose . . .
And for the sons and daughters, and families,
whose lives were lost or changed forever
by the school shootings.

ACKNOWLEDGMENTS

The topic of this book, *Cliques*, seemed to hit a note with everyone wherever we traveled, on business or pleasure, to another city or in our own neighborhoods. Parents of young adolescents, of course, talked about present struggles with their children because these battles are current and painful. Others we met, however, went back to their own childhoods to tell us tales of being excluded, taunted, or bullied. One friend spoke about the misery she had suffered in fifth grade at the hands of the classroom bully, Roberta, whose nickname, "Butchie," seemed to say it all. Years later, this friend was shocked when she met at a party one of Butchie's co-conspirators, who couldn't remember being in a clique. "How could I feel the sting all these years later and yet she has no memory of being so mean?" this woman asked. That story and others convinced us of the long-lasting hurt inflicted by cliques and helped us redouble our efforts to bring the topic to the forefront so that our own children won't bear such social scars.

Working on this book also brought home to us the true meaning of friendship. This book is the third one we have co-authored together and each venture grows more enjoyable. We are business associates, yes, but our friendship continues to grow and we are grateful for that gift.

We are also grateful for the many people who have helped us along the way. Once again, we thank John Lounsbury of the National Middle School Association, who has been so supportive. We are continually amazed at his ability to inspire us and others with his knowledge, kindness, and most of all his wisdom. The parents we have met while giving talks around the country provided the impetus for this work. The administrators, principals, teachers, social workers, and school nurses who added their thoughts are much appreciated.

Our electronic sandbox, "Parent Soup," has helped us to stay in touch with parents all over the United States and, indeed, the world. We would like to thank Susan Hahn, Faith Maupin, and Tammy Prather for all the attention they devote to our sites on America Online and the web. We also would like to thank our regular chatters, our friends in cyberspace, who bring us their problems, but also bring us their ideas.

Our editor, Luke Dempsey, connected with our idea immediately, having his own stories to tell about going to school in England. He brought his understanding and considerable talents as an editor to this book, helping us sharpen our manuscript. Under his hand our passion came across brighter. His assistant, Amanda Gross, was never too busy to handle any detail. We haven't forgotten our former editor, Tracy Behar, who initially bought this book and placed us in Luke's expert hands. A special thanks to her. And to Debbie Stier, publicity director, who has cheered us on from the outset. Her enthusiasm is contagious and affects everyone who enters her circle. We also would like to thank Brian Jones in publicity, who continues to publicize all of our books.

To our agent and friend, Denise Marcil, who deftly steers us through the ever-changing landscape of publishing, our deepest appreciation. She manages to find the perfect venues for us, whether on paper or in cyberspace.

Finally, to all our friends. We have many and we are grateful for all they do to enrich our lives, ease our burdens, and make us laugh.

CONTENTS

CLIQUES

Introduction

Conquering the Cruel Climate That Dominates Our Schools

Recently we'd delivered a talk in Long Island, New York, and afterward a mother backed us up against the wall, pleading:

—"My twelve-year-old son clicked on an e-mail that read, 'I'm going to kill you.' We know the bully who sent it. He's been picking on my son all year, and others, too. The principal brushed me off with a 'Don't worry—these kids' barks are worse than their bites' speech. I'm angry, I'm frustrated, and most of all I'm worried. What should I do?"

From cyberspace another mom e-mailed our site:

—"My eleven-year-old son is being tormented mercilessly by two classmates who are also teammates on his baseball team. After months of tears and angst every day, it erupted into an attack on the playground. My son is stronger and kept pushing them away. I called the school and the other parents. That's only made things worse for my son, called 'Crybaby' ever since by everyone. Now what?"

After a book signing outside Baltimore, a mother and father took us aside:

—"Our fifteen-year-old tells lies all over the place. She's in a new school this year. The girls there are all jealous of her, she says. Our daughter is very pretty and athletic. Fitting in at such a cliquish school apparently is rough. Could this be affecting her self-esteem and triggering the lying?"

A friend of a friend telephones for help:

—"My nice, pretty seventh-grader has no friends. She eats alone in the cafeteria, she walks alone in the halls. She says it is like she is a ghost. She does not know what she has done wrong. Needless to say, she's depressed and said last night that she would like to kill herself. My husband and I are at a loss as to what to do. Can you suggest something—*anything?*"

We wish we could tell you that these questions about clique activity and bullying are exceptions. We cannot. We hear tales of torture and torment every single day: "My child can't break into the cliques," or "My child can't break away from the infighting." As we travel we have conversations about victimized boys and girls like these all the time with mothers, fathers, and with young adolescents themselves. From parents on-line we hear indictments, sometimes half a dozen a day. Cliques rule. Bullying is epidemic. We've heard this over and over again even from our own children and we have the cracks in our hearts to prove as much.

Every day in *every* school in *every* community all across this country, children are cut down. A boy's pants are pulled down in the locker room for sport. A girl who just kicked an assist so her teammate could score a soccer goal is shunned hours later by that same teammate. This is not the bra-snapping or "boys will be boys" wrestling you recall from your own youth. Today, girls are obscenely maligned, groped, and intimidated. Boys are assaulted physically and emotionally with an endless stream of taunts.

We can give you proof. Researcher Charol Shakeshaft of Hofstra University surveyed 1,000 middle and high school students by asking them one open-ended question: "What's it really like in school?" The universal answer turned out to be that school is a miserable place because of all the teasing and bullying. Do you want to hear more? According to the Education Foundation of the American Association of University Women, four out of five adolescents in 1,600 public schools across the country said sexual harassment, bullying with sexual overtones, is widespread.

Statistics aside, the most important proof is right there in the lives of your children. Ask them. They will tell you about the cliques. They will introduce you to the ringleaders. They will testify about the bullying that goes on. It's their life.

Just drive by any bus stop in the morning. Elementary school children are bouncing and laughing. Middle school children are not. They wait for that bus in silence without looking each another in the eye. Why? Each is steeling himself or herself for the first gauntlet of the day: walking down the aisle of the school bus. Boys get tripped. Girls hear mean-spirited giggling after they pass. Baseball caps are ripped off unsuspecting heads. Some can't find a welcome seat. Why do you think your middler asks, "Mom, can't you drive me to school? I hate taking the bus."

That's how our young adolescents start the day. Then they get to go inside the school. Let the games begin—bodies being slammed into lockers, backpacks being tossed, and girls backstabbing one another. Let's not leave out the sound of silence, the sound of being shunned. Classes such as algebra or global studies follow. Everyone is paying attention, less to the teacher standing in front, more to notes passing between classmates carrying the shorthand of who's in, who's out, and who's getting the silent treatment. Sneers, leers, looks, and cutting remarks keep everyone well aware of their place. When it's time for lunch, almost everyone feels pangs of anxiety alongside hunger pangs. The menu of being judged, called names, or exiled would make you lose your appetite, too. And so it goes.

Oh come on, you may be thinking. Aren't we exaggerating? Is it that bad?

No. It's not *that* bad. It's worse. We have not heard from every child or every parent.

If you think that we are not talking about *your* child, you are naive. If your child has never confided to you that he has been victimized, that doesn't mean he hasn't. It only means he has not shared his painful story with you. Furthermore, no child is going to volunteer that she just made another girl's day pure misery. She won't repeat to you all the deliciously vicious lies she spread to ruin another girl's reputation.

In the climate of cruelty that thrives in today's schools and peaks during middle school, everybody's child suffers. Even mothers of the prettiest girls in the class have complained. A well-heeled Chicago mom confessed that her beautiful sixth-grade daughter cries in her room nightly, afraid she will won't look *right* tomorrow and as a consequence she will lose her standing. A popular fourteen-year-old admitted that she slashed her arm with a wallpaper cutter to bleed out the shame she felt after hearing rumors accusing her of sleeping around. The smartest boy in a seventh-grade class in Ohio told us that his homework is his only refuge. A teacher in Lake Placid reported that her smart thirteen-year-old son had announced, "Mom, I'm going to fail that science test tomorrow. I just have to or I won't have any friends." A fifteen-year-old girl from Minnesota said she deliberately ruined her shapely body by gaining fifteen pounds and hiding beneath loose-fitting shirts so the boys would stop humiliating her.

Why the Worst Behavior?

Why are young adolescents acting this way? We didn't raise our children to be this mean! The answer lies in some combination of nature and nurture.

Human development plays a significant part. Infants and young children need to be loved by their parents because family is their whole world. As children move into early adolescence, their world view expands. They discover the world of peers. Now they need to be liked by those peers. Having one friend proves a child is liked. More friends prove a child is even more highly esteemed. Popularity becomes the measure of likeability. Becoming popular, arguing about who is popular and who isn't—these issues become an obsession for ten- to fifteen-year-olds.

Since every child wants to be popular, you would think each would put her best foot forward and be on her best behavior. That can happen of course. Some boys and girls win friends and earn the esteem of their peers legitimately. However, others pursue popularity illegitimately. They opt for control to ensure they have friends around, reaching for popularity's golden ring by knocking down the competition. They grab power by intimidating others or by fighting for it. These attempts at getting a fan club, these seizures of power, character assassinations, and physical brutality illustrate the worst misbehaviors. These children not only get away with such behavior, but they set a low standard which is invariably copied by others.

Why don't the good children or the good instincts prevail? The need to be liked, and to acquire friends to prove as much, isn't the only development issue on a middler's plate. During early adolescence children are also trying to figure out: Who am I? Who will I become? Their bodies are growing and changing. So are their brains. Struggling with this emerging identity is taxing. It makes all middlers fragile, self-conscious, and insecure. Unsure of themselves, they become timid and vulnerable. They resist making waves. That's why when a middler sees a classmate targeted, she is afraid to object. There is a big risk in defending a victim. Power-hungry types capitalize on their peer's insecurities.

The climate of cruelty is about human nature; it's also about nurturing, or rather, the lack thereof. Many of us work more and spend less time with our children. A child who turns ten, eleven, or twelve is allowed to spend more time unsupervised and in the company of peers. Experts warn that we have become negligent and have left our young to their own devices too much of the time. Authors cast adolescents today as a tribe apart, directionless and dangerous. Books like *The Nurture Assumption* claim that our influence is limited and that our adolescents actually mold one another.

There's plenty to debate there. What isn't debatable is the well-defined youth culture that surrounds our children and affects them. Today's young adolescents have their own culture complete with a television network, Nickelodeon, their own music, language, celebrities, and a world of material goods aggressively advertised to them at every turn. They are a world unto themselves.

Along with the rest of society, that youth culture is rougher and tougher. There is more violence acted out everywhere on and off TV, movie, and video screens. Cursing has reached new highs, or should we say new lows. Put-downs and sarcasm are routinely written into nearly every

TV sitcom. Talk shows feature endless combinations of people betraying or abusing one another. All of these factors—nature, nurture, and culture—have created a climate where mean-spiritedness is not only accepted but cultivated.

This Climate of Cruelty Is Fixable

There is good news, however. Things can be turned around. We decided to do something to fight back against the toxic atmosphere in middle schools after visiting communities coast to coast to talk about our books, *The Roller-Coaster Years: Raising Your Child Through the Maddening Yet Magical Middle School Years* and *Parenting* 911. We had to do something to address the suffering we heard and also witnessed firsthand in our own families. In 1997, we began giving a workshop called "With Friends Like These" to middle school students. Our goal was to bring this cruelty out into the open and arm young adolescents with the awareness and skills to handle cliques, bullies, and teasing.

Word of our effort spread. Parents began sneaking into the sessions, lobbying for us to teach them about these issues as well. In response, we created a similar workshop for parents, and other customized versions tailored to teachers, health care professionals in the schools like social workers, and administrators. In Hartford, Connecticut, several of the Girl Scouts in our audience burst into tears and ran out of the gymnasium as we talked about the sting of certain words. Moments like that showed us how poignantly and effectively we strike the right nerves.

A turning point for us, along with the nation, turned out to be the school massacre in Littleton, Colorado, on April 20, 1999. High school misfits Eric Harris and Dylan Klebold shot twelve peers, one teacher, and then took their own lives. We'd been out to that exact community six months prior to do a book signing at the local Barnes & Noble. With the wisdom of hindsight, we wished that we had had the opportunity to deliver our workshop to that community's adolescent population.

It's too late to save all the victims of the rash of school shootings over the last few years. We can't bring them back. It's not too late to save our own children from being victimized or driven to outrageous acts by cruelty and rage. We can create a healthier atmosphere for our young people.

Educators wax on about higher standards in academics. The best classroom lesson on earth cannot be grasped by a student who is distracted by a more pressing and stressing agenda: Cliques 101. Psychologists coach us about how to build up fragile self-esteem and recognize the signs of adolescent depression, yet they fail to identify the culprit of shattered self-image: peer to peer harassment. Principals talk about safety issues. Legislators talk about gun control. Politicians and district attorneys debate juvenile offender statutes. No one addresses the root cause of school violence: a steady diet of debilitating ridicule. Social isolation and humiliation fuel rage. Certain adolescent boys fill up with anger until they explode. For the susceptible female equivalent, humiliation can turn to despondency and erupt in adolescent suicide.

We must all become emotional enough and mad enough to take action. Parents have admitted to us "I've wanted to strangle that child for saying those things about my daughter!" We've harbored revenge fantasies, too, and had to manage our anger. We have felt deep sadness at the experiences of our children and other people's children. We are ready. Are you?

It's got to stop. We have to put an end to the fourth "R," ridicule, that is right alongside the other three in our schools—reading, writing, and arithmetic. The subject has been bottled up inside our children for too long. The taunting has been a silent shame, a national scandal, for too long. This book is a mandate to change the climate in our schools from cruel to kind. Ours is a call to arms that emphasizes reaching out with our arms to our children to help them battle cliques. What you will encounter in the following pages is an action plan. Step by step you will learn how to help your child bring to the surface what's been happening out of the earshot and eyesight of adults. You will be schooled in what to say and what to do to change your child's experiences and self-image and discover a blueprint to transform your child's world. One parent at a time, one child at a time, one community at a time, we can cure the social disease that has been running wild.

School, and especially middle school, is supposed to be a place where our children are nurtured. As we stand at the dawn of a new millennium, human nature has taken a turn for the meaner. In response, we have to cultivate a higher standard of compassion and tolerance. It's time for new values, a resurrection of our best old values, and a fresh commitment. Together we can tame the social jungle in which our children have become lost.

Let's start a dialogue with our children about all the rules that govern their lives—where she sits in the cafeteria, whom he picks during gym class, which children she can smile at, which girls he can flirt with. Who makes these rules? It is not us, the parents. It is not the teachers. The rules are made by fifth-graders. A few fifth-graders get classmates willingly and unwillingly to play certain roles and the rest conspire in the ongoing drama. The rules continue through middle school and into high school, rules made by ten-year-olds. Our children can shatter them.

At the anniversary of the Littleton, Colorado, massacre, *New York Newsday* reported that one high school senior by the name of Sara Blackford who survived that tragedy is still worried: "Is there another student secretly plotting to kill me and my classmates?" That wasn't the worst of what she said. She added: "I kind of expected things to change between people after Columbine, that they would be more respectful and not make fun of people. But that didn't happen."

Our children can't be expected to turn the tide of teasing and of clique cruelty around all by themselves. We have to show them how. We have to take the time to work with them to loosen the straitjackets, soften the talk, and open up their hearts.

STEP ONE

Help Your Child Belong

A need to belong emerges with a vengeance during early adolescence, a period we choose to mean the ages from ten through fifteen. This is when your child discovers that a whole world exists beyond the family: peers. That social realm commands more and more attention. An overwhelming desire to fit in takes center stage. Your child's thoughts and reactions revolve around her interests with friends and peers. Friends are supposed to ease the passage from childhood toward adulthood. Of course, that's not always the way it works out.

This shift away from parents and family is a natural one. To make that journey toward independence less lonely, young adolescents latch onto one another. Having a tight-knit bunch of friends makes going to school fun for a middler. A band of friends provides a home away from home. Your child's peers become his allies and accomplices.

A young adolescent's lot is to figure out who she is. The peer group serves as a panel. It helps members define themselves. Groups have identifiable clothing, music, activities, inside jokes, and rituals. Buddy systems evolve, sifting boys and girls with similar interests neatly into categories. That is not to say that this process is all fun and games.

As peers divide up, children form into cliques. The term "clique" is used loosely to define a particular group of friends, but more often to define a group that revolves around more than camaraderie. Cliques deal in social power. Formed around a leader or two, the pack lets it be known that *not* everybody is welcome. Certain children are dubbed "worthy" while others are judged "not good enough." Excluding becomes a primary activity. The mentality is like a junior country club. The guest list to this invitation-only party is always changing.

The way cliques operate in middle school creates a great deal of distress. Controlling personalities rise to the top. Unsuspecting young adolescents become targets for the more powerful and popular clique members to ridicule, and free-roaming bullies who don't fit anywhere add to the climate. Belittling others solidifies power. Our young collide with a closed caste system. Peers are pigeonholed by one another. Very quickly, many, if not all, lose their social innocence.

Cliques and peer groups have strict rules. These are rules

not made to be broken. Who to talk to, sit with, dress like; if you act out of sync with your band, you are going to be criticized. Since all young adolescents are supersensitive to criticism, many have difficulty standing up for themselves or for what's right. So cliques rule. Certain children get away with emotionally tormenting many. The fitting-in dance is often excruciating.

Yet even though establishing a place in the peer group is riddled with danger, every middler still needs to find that sense of belonging. This is where you can really be of assistance. In this chapter, we'll be showing you how to help your child find that sense of belonging in healthy and positive ways. We will show you how to:

- Validate your child's need to join the group without leaving your influence behind.
- Lead your child on a few information-gathering missions to give her a social edge.
- Peek inside a few diaries to teach her some surprising truths.
- Offer a daily dose of "belonging instructions."

Think of this first step as another verse to that old Crosby, Stills, Nash, and Young classic song "Love the One You're With." Maybe your child can't be with the ones she loves, and even covets, but she can learn to love the ones she's with. It's all in the way she look at things, and at herself and her choices.

Letting Go . . . and Being There

You can't accompany your ten-, eleven-, or twelve-year-old child as she gets her social bearings. You can't sit with her on the bus when no one else will, nor can you whisper witty jokes in her ear on Friday night so that she becomes the life of the sleep over party. If only we could override the trial and error process of finding the right social fit.

Even though you realize this, don't assume that you have no role whatsoever in your child's social awakening. Your child needs you *more than ever* as she ventures out on this quest to find her place in her world. Too often parents fail to grasp their new role. They confuse letting go with checking out. Your new role begins with reinforcing your child's socializing drive.

How? Here are a few common mistakes to avoid:

1. *Don't dismiss social turmoil as petty.* At some point, if you haven't already, you probably will hear these words come from your middler's mouth: "Everyone makes fun of me!" Or you may encounter a deafening silence, no explanation for that bruise your son comes home with on his cheek. Or your daughter will be inconsolable over remarks made behind her back, maybe even by her best friend.

Once upon a time, mothers and fathers pooh-poohed these social tornadoes as just part of growing up. Getting ridiculed in the locker room or hearing your so-called friends chop you down behind your back—such experiences garnered standard advice: "Deal with it." Or "Honey, just ignore it."

Responding to a crisis with turn-a-deaf-ear advice doesn't help. Nor does tuning out because you don't have a better snippet of wisdom. Your child needs your full attention. Encourage her to tell you more, not less. Empathize with how painful trying to fit in can be. Finessing social acceptance is all about learning social intelligence. Reassure your fledging ugly duckling that she will get her sea legs socially with time. Tuning in, telling your child to turn up the volume of her complaints validates her struggles to fit in. It replenishes her spirit when she needs it most.

2. *Don't give your child the message that you resent her newfound friends.* Ask yourself these questions: When your child rebuffs your invitation to go to a movie on Friday night (because she'd rather stay on-line instant messaging her friends), do you act hurt? Is the tip of your tongue smarting with warnings about that boy's fresh mouth or that girl's skin-tight tube top?

Your behavior either encourages or discourages your child from socializing with peers. Our young adolescents are driven to their friends, yet they secretly (and sometimes not so secretly) long for our permission and our approval of their social desires. We will never be able to help them develop good instincts about friends if they feel we never give any of their chosen buddies a chance. If you subtly or openly do nothing but reject your middler's friendships, he won't share information on that side of himself with you after school or after a party.

Greet your daughter's pals with an open mind. Make your son's cohorts feel welcome in your home. Show by your attitude that you endorse your child's need to fit into a group. Otherwise you are backing your child into a corner, forcing her to choose between your approval or her friends' acceptance. For a twelve- or thirteen-year-old that is a non-choice. We don't have to tell you that friends will win hands down.

With simple gestures like waiting up when a child comes home or checking in after school, you make yourself available and eager to hear about your child's new life. Every chat about who's going out with whom creates a safe haven where your child can review the social steps or missteps of the day.

3. *Don't overrate social successes or obsess over social failures.* With some children it's easy to go overboard with compliments. "I can't believe how many boys congratulated you on your jump shot." Other parents feel they must always be on the lookout to protect a child. "I saw the way that snob ignored you when you sat down next to her on the bench at the soccer game." Being stuck in either extreme sends a sabotaging message; a child either hears that he is perfect and nothing less is expected, or she hears that she is socially incompetent.

Of course, it's natural to want to reinforce a child's social coups and make up for social slights. However, children need help processing both kinds of social experiences. Here's one idea: every day at dinner or at bedtime, ask: "What's the best thing that happened today?" and "What's the worst thing that happened today?" Then listen as she reports the good, the bad, and the ugly. Let her know that both negative and positive episodes happen. And tell her you love her either way.

Diagram the Cafeteria

Let's be honest with one another. Not all of our sons or daughters can be crowned most popular, rated best looking or smartest, or wind up captain of the lacrosse team or star of the musical. Although we can't finagle a middler the coveted top spots of the middle school heap, we can help each locate a spot for himself. Furthermore, we can change the way our children perceive themselves and their place on the social ladder.

The starting point lies in guiding your child on an information-gathering mission. Remember diagramming sentences in English class? On a straight horizontal line you wrote noun (subject). Next to it, you penned the action word, the verb (predicate). Adverbs veered off underneath on a diagonal line. In the world of grammar, every word in the English language has its place.

Now let's give this exercise a new life. A middle school cafeteria converts naturally into a neatly diagrammed sentence; you can go into any one in any part of the country and see social order. Each and every munching middler knows exactly on *which* table in *what* part of the room to set down a lunch tray.

Ask your child to diagram the cafeteria by describing to

you each of the different cliques or groups in her class. If your child is willing, let her write a list of the groups on paper. Or if she is so inclined, she may want to literally draw the lunchroom layout labeling the cliques. If she's artistic, encourage her to draw caricatures. The freaks could get blue spiky hairdos. The preppies could be accessorized with pom-poms. The jocks might sport bouncing balls under the metal picnic tables. One way or another, the goal is to get her to recognize the caste system that exists in her school.

Wait a minute. How will you know if she's doing this right? How can you be sure she includes the total cross-section of types? In order to prepare you, here is the typical breakdown of middle school according to Colorado sociologists Patricia and Peter Adler, who are also co-authors of *Peer Power: Preadolescent Culture and Identity.* They documented the classic social order by stalking their own children's community of third to sixth graders over a period of eight years. Boys and girls throughout these grades sifted themselves into clear-cut categories, and the dividing lines were based on peer status. The Adlers' meticulous examination of the cafeteria set dovetails with what other researchers have turned up. Here's our shorthand based on their four basic groups:

The Popular Clique This is the cool group. The beautiful, the athletic, the charming, the affluent; these middlers combine to make up about 35% of the population. These children have the most friends, socialize earlier than others inside and outside of school, and appear to be having all the fun. Above all, they have prestige. Their romances, scholastic achievements, and athletic exploits command everyone's attention, including teachers and classmates. This exclusive top rung leads and sets the tone for the entire class.

The Fringe About 10% of children hover around the popular set. These boys and girls mimic the dress and the rules set by the top caste. Occasionally, leaders of the popular clique let them come in and play, but only temporarily. The fringers accept their part-time superiority because running with the "in crowd" some of the time is worth being left behind the rest of the time. It's a new twist on that old adage that half a loaf is better than none.

Middle Friendship Circles The majority of boys and girls, nearly half at 45%, form small groups of several friends apiece. They carry on with their daily lives with assorted measures of confidence and satisfaction. These circles opt for a look and a culture of their own making. A 1999 *Time* magazine article ticked off a long list of categories ranging from geeks, skateboarders, nerds, and hockey kids, to stoners, gangbangers, Abercrombies, Goths, and hootchies. These solid, wholesome, or alternative subgroups realize they are labeled unpopular. Some care. Others refuse to play the popularity game. It should be said, though, that nearly all feel some resentment or even contempt for the popular group whose shenanigans and high-profile exploits are impossible to ignore.

The Loners These are the boys and girls who have no friends. Usually 10% of a class falls into this category.

Social hermits sit alone in the cafeteria or languish in the hallways watching and envying the ones who seem to belong so naturally.

Keep these tiers in mind as you have your child tick off the different categories. We have given this exercise a trial run among the many groups of middlers we've addressed over the past several years. They get it. Let your middler show you the social order. Get a dialogue going about some of the personalities. What about that little boy who used to be your daughter's best friend in preschool? Where did he land? You might even get out some old class photographs or snapshots from yesteryear's kiddie birthday parties.

In a variation of "What Ever Happened To . . . ?" let your middler update you. You will be surprised, and often entertained, as you are reintroduced to children you have known since kindergarten or those you have lost track of. That little nature nut, the girl who once led your child into the woods to capture butterflies with a net, has metamorphasized into a girl who is capturing hearts in the woods behind the elementary school (good thing your son isn't as close to her as he used to be). Who would have ever thought that the shy, frail wisp of a boy from second grade would wind up captain of the football team? Back then the prediction looked more like "Most Likely to Get Stuffed Regularly into a Locker!"

Move the exercise along to which boys and girls are in control of the clique activity. Have your child identify the leaders. Does one personality hold all the power in the popular crowd or is it shared? Invite your child to explain the criteria for admission to a clique. Is it a matter of style? Is there a "uniform?" Have her detail the typical outfit for each group. What stores supply the looks? The Gap? Abercrombie and Fitch? Thrift-shop chic?

Play a matching game with the categories. What are most groups known for? Do student government meetings after school pack in the popular clique? Are the stoners lurking outside the gate at 7:30 A.M., getting that first hit of cigarette smoke before the first bell? Who is always in the computer lab? The band room? We guarantee that you will be treated to a lively introduction to the caste system. Young adolescents *always* gossip, vent, lampoon, and criticize the cliques to one another. Rarely do they get the opportunity to dazzle the adults in their lives with such in-depth knowledge of their social order. Adults aren't usually part of it, and don't work at understanding this aspect of their children's lives.

Along the way to explaining the social grid, inevitably your child will tell you where he fits in. Perhaps you already know. Perhaps you aren't sure, or have been afraid to find out. Hold all your reservations aside for the moment. Just listen, learn, and watch your child unfold his social expertise. Make sure you tell your daughter how impressed you are with her powers of observation. Empathize when she groans about the injustices of the powers that be. Above all, get the point across that your child is anything but a social know-nothing no matter where her fate falls on the social ladder. Therein lies the beauty and the power of this information-gathering session.

Here's what to take away from these discussions:

- A child who learns to recognize the categories within the school population benefits from feeling socially aware and acknowledges how adept she is at reading the social landscape.
- A child who puts every name and face into a group realizes that there is a group for every face and name. Labels, on the one hand, do pigeonhole; yet on the other hand, they deliver a sense of fitting in somewhere.
- A child with keen powers of observation is ready to look further. The caste system isn't exactly what it appears to be.

Clique Patrol . . . The Winners and the Losers

Make no mistake. Your child's self-image is affected by where he fits in both inside and outside the cafeteria. All labels either enhance or chip away at a middler's developing self-esteem. Don't forget that the caste system has a definite pecking order. Without much egging on your child will rank the cliques from the top to the bottom. It becomes obvious who's in and who's not.

How does your child feel about her place in the crowd? Is she proud of her assigned spot in the cafeteria, or embarrassed? Does she look at her own group as a bunch of losers or second-string players? Is your attractive daughter arrogant, even turning off you, her parent, with her ice-queen pride? Is your son a member of the golden club of hotshots and heading for a fall?

No matter where your child is in the cafeteria hierarchy, there are advantages and disadvantages. The stereotypical winners don't always feel or act like winners. And the supposed losers have winning characteristics. This isn't always understood by our young adolescents. As your child leads you on this guided tour of popularity city, pay attention to what he believes. In all likelihood your child envies the popular girls and boys because they seem to get everything that's fun—from love letters to top billing in yearbooks to recognition from teachers. Children who dwell in the twosomes or threesomes, revolving around alternative music or marching band, miss the perks of higher and cooler ground. The fact is that each and every category carries within it both positive and negative features.

Getting this message across bolsters, humbles, and stretches every child's self-image. Stress to your child that even popular boys and girls are prone to anxieties and unhappiness. Furthermore, those children who look like they have little to offer hold promise that may not show itself during middle school or even high school. Reassure your child that every one of his classmates struggles and suffers. The secrets aren't always written on their peers' faces. Beneath all masks is insecurity. And some masks obscure truths.

The Whirl of the Society Pages Versus Dear Diary

Sometimes you may find it difficult to change your child's ideas about those *lucky* popular children or those *unlucky* uncool ones. So let's go look more closely into each of the categories that the Adlers scoped out. It's like peeking into the diaries of the jocks or the skateboarders. What you will see is the other side of the stereotype. This little exercise will give you insights that you can point out to your child, and these observations will get your child thinking that people are not always whom they appear to be.

Chances are that she has not made these discoveries on her own:

The popular child's diary reads "I'm always worried."

Within the "A" crowd, there is constant jockeying. Who's *in* and who's *on the outs* changes day-to-day, even hour by hour. A kind of "follow the clique-leader" game produces constant anxiety. As the Adlers observed, "Followers suffered through their subordination to the leaders by being bossed around, derided, and stigmatized, and by frequently worrying about losing their position in the group. Members of the group did not share positive identity." In other words, these popular children didn't necessarily feel good about themselves *inside* even if they looked good on the outside or had the admiration of their peers.

Furthermore, being on the social party circuit is full of drawbacks. Young adolescents who socialize more often face temptation to engage in risky behavior sooner and more frequently. This young adolescent girl's comments make a sobering point. "The first day of sixth grade my number one goal was to be really cool. I yearned to be accepted by that clique—always together laughing and smiling so proud. An imaginary wall surrounded them, making them ideal, the best. By eighth grade I was popular and well-liked. I had tried hard, finally arrived. Or so I thought. I discovered my so-called friends were not quality people. Hooking up with guys all the time, partying, drinking, drugging, not trying at schoolwork. I saw firsthand the trashing of anyone who didn't want to go along with the crowd." Yes, the term "party animal" has a dark side.

The fringe child's diary reads, "Where's my self-respect?"

The common name for this fringe set is "wannabe." If your child isn't one of those wannabes, when she tells you about these "suck-ups to the popular crowd," you will hear her pity. Why do so many boys and girls almost feel sorry for the fringe set? Because these middlers are always swallowing their pride. They are willing to trade their self-respect for part-time popularity. The Adlers remark, "They (the wannabes) desperately aspired to be accepted by people who toyed with them, using them for their own benefit. They suffered by always desiring something that they never really attained, enduring the frustration of experiencing it temporarily only to lose it again. They knew that the people they wanted as friends did not want them, and mocked, teased, and derided them."

The fringers have to live under illusions all the time. They want the popular children to become their friends, and at times, they succeed—almost. Deep down, though, fringers know the truth and the pain of being almost, but never quite, good enough. The friends they drop in a second to answer the call of the clique leader are the ones they should be appreciating.

In the friendship circles, the child's diary reads, "I'm free and content."

These children are outside the cool group and have lower status. At times they are teased. Yet their lives and relationships have wonderful commodities, namely security and loyalty. Neither of these are part and parcel for the popular crowd. The clique drama queens and kings rarely feel secure for very long. The loyalty they claim isn't stable. Because it's won by manipulating and intimidating others, it is always in flux.

Another bonus of friendship circles is personal freedom. Consider this situation: What happens to a new kid at school? In the popular clique, you can't just bring a new face to the lunch table, not without the permission of the leader of the pack. If you do, it's against the rules and you will have to watch out for ridicule. For children in the friendship circles, the exact opposite holds true. The middle schoolers in this category, be they geeks or nerds, have the freedom to include someone new. Not being exclusive in nature has its advantages. These boys and girls can think for themselves and explore relationships.

Here's a pivotal question to ask your child: Which group tends to have the most reliable and rewarding friendships?

Correct your child with this truth. Children in these smaller circles do. These less popular children may not have an "A" list of party animals in their e-mail address books, but they can trust the friends they make.

The loner child's diary reads, "I'm mad and I can't take it anymore."

Don't be horrified if you hear your outspoken rebel or shy wallflower say she relates to the gun-toting perpetrators of tragic school shooting scenarios. In a 1999 *Seventeen* magazine cover story on cliques, an otherwise ordinary teenager confessed, "Because of my own experience with vicious in-crowd members, my sympathies lay with Eric Harris and Dylan Klebold (the Columbine shooters)."

Children who are repeatedly isolated accumulate a great deal of pain. If a child is insulted by more popular peers every day for years on end, he carries around a burden of bad feelings. The weight of rejection is heavy. It makes a young adolescent devalue his or her own worth. A child in this uncool prison can become enraged with those who levy insults at him without provocation or punishment. Some will make remarks like those in *Seventeen* magazine in order to get the anger that develops from that pain off their chests. For most, these words are not harbingers of violence. Yet there are a few middlers who indeed bear watching.

That's why it is so important for the parents of socially isolated young adolescents to recognize their plight. These young adolescents need attention or they are susceptible to adolescent depression, drug abuse, or moving into violent subcultures (for parents who suspect their child is in this predicament a more detailed game plan will be presented in Step Four that focuses on victims).

There is some good news about this group. Maybe their lives don't revolve around a social whirl of parties, but that fate has a surprising benefit. Think of Bill Gates who admits he was an unpopular geeky outcast. These children probably have a hidden talent or unrecognized potential, plus they have time to devote to that skill or to hone that talent. Parents need to help such a child identify hidden assets and find ways to mine that ability.

Before you close all of these diaries, ask your child this final question: Which category or clique tends to include children with the best self-image? Give her time to debate the issue. Listen as she weighs the assets against the liabilities of the people she watches every day in school. Hopefully, she'll put what she has learned from the diaries into her conclusion.

Then unveil the truth. Children in the middle, in friendship circles, tend to feel most content. "Individuals in the middle group generally felt good about themselves," the Adlers concluded. Why? Being able to count on loyalty from their friends and not living with so much anxiety adds up to a healthier self-image and higher self-esteem. The popular types tend to wear anxiety along with the latest fashions. The fringers live in a state of second best. They hear a running inner dialogue of second thoughts. Isolated middlers are sentenced to loneliness and rejection.

After this exercise, your child will realize that things

aren't always what they seem. The winners don't all, or always, feel like winners. The less popular are not losing out on as much as they might think. The truth is that no one in middle school has it made. If your son or daughter wanted to trade places with someone higher up on the middle school food chain, we bet second thoughts are cropping up. You can't change what clique your child is in, but you can change the way she feels about cliques.

The Lunch Bag Chronicles

Belonging cannot be achieved alone. Your child has to choose friends. While the friends saga is an ongoing drama in which you are an onlooker, here is one final strategy in which you can play a major role. This method of enhancing your child's sense of belonging came to us quite by accident. Busy working mothers of young adolescents ourselves, we started to slip little notes in our daughters' lunches. We'd pack a trio of lunches in advance of leaving for a series of lectures and try to compensate for our absence by writing these reminders. They appeared trite at first glance: "Have a nice day" or "Hope that English test was easier than you thought." Both of our daughters loved our little lunch box chronicles packed alongside the chips, Gatorade, and peanut butter and jelly sandwiches.

When we mentioned this anecdote to other parents, many chimed in with knowing endorsement. They, too, had added words of encouragement to the bagels and cream cheese ensembles. Their middle school sons and daughters responded enthusiastically to these notes, even if they didn't broadcast the contents to the rest of the bologna and cheese set.

Middlers crave our attention. They love little reminders from us because in this way they are reminded of how much we care. These emotional recipes pack a hefty punch. Something as simple as this ritual provides you with an excellent opportunity to build your child's sense of belonging, positively, one day at a time. Feature these in a note along with, or even written on, the napkin.

Flash a smile.
Return a smile.
Pass a note of encouragement to a friend.
Compliment someone on their shirt, hair, baggies.
Save someone a seat on the bus.
Comment positively on a creative doodle on someone's notebook or backpack.
Stop at someone's locker and admire how cleverly it's decorated inside.
Congratulate another on a poem well-written, an opinion well-spoken.
Say "hi" to someone when you pass them in the hall.
Choose someone for a teammate in gym.
Volunteer to partner with someone for a class project.
Offer to help a struggling student with that math homework.
Invite someone to get off the bus with you to work on your homework.

Stay after school to watch the basketball game.
Tell a player the day after a game, a math competition, a spelling bee, you thought he or she did really well.

Ask your child what makes him feel like he belongs. Recycle that tip in next month's lunch sack.

The Legacy of Belonging

A child needs acceptance in order to feel good. At this age, the crowd is like a mirror. When acceptance is withheld, a child assumes she is somehow lacking. When rejection is levied, a middler takes the blame personally. The psychic damage is imprinted on a highly fragile and struggling self-image. The squeeze may happen to a ten-, eleven-, or twelve-year-old, but the repercussions reverberate for a lifetime.

Trying to achieve and balance that sense of belonging is a fundamental early adolescent milestone. It's not just about being popular in fourth grade or being a shoo-in on the guest list in seventh. Recognizing the importance of developing this skill is preparing your child with indispensable equipment for life.

Whether a child survives and succeeds isn't simply a fate that can make or break his middle school experience. Knowing how to find and take one's place is critical in college, in the workplace, in the neighborhood, in the community, in virtually every group a person encounters for the rest of life. The friendships that children make during early adolescence are the ones that are the most indelible. Your middler has to find that sense of belonging herself, but you are an indispensable, albeit invisible, ally. As a parent you are both impotent and potent.

The Ultimate Acceptance

There is a difference between social and personal acceptance. Finding one's personal identity is different than living with one's social identity. Children need to distinguish between the two at this age. They need our guidance.

The "*Who am I?*" quest is a personal assignment. What the group decrees is not the final verdict. "*Who are you?*" is a process of discovery that happens within the walls of your child's bedroom. The answers she hears in the hallways are not the opinions that ultimately matter.

Alone is a reality that our sons and daughters are not as comfortable with during early adolescence. It's up to us as parents to lead them there. Talk about individual goals and performance. Inspire self-discovery. Define integrity as personal character and living according to a code of values. Integrity and personal dignity are commodities that cannot be taken away by anyone, even the most popular or powerful peer. These can only be surrendered.

Social acceptance is another issue and a very important one to our young adolescents. In your talks, your middler should get the message that fitting in hinges on conformity. Since the crowd looks glorious to our middlers, tarnishing its image is useful. The group has expectations. You want your child to consider what she is giving up. Is she forfeiting an extra hour's sleep to spend time in front of the mirror? Is he cloning himself? Is she biting her tongue? Is he stifling his conscience? The duel boils down to two different concepts: alone and clone.

Cliques wield power, but not all the power. It is the middler's personal power that grants the clique its power. Every act of going along, agreeing, not disagreeing, is a personal decision that either strengthens or challenges cliques. To your young adolescent child, peers are the jury. Your child often feels like the plaintiff but he is really the judge. While your son or daughter struggles with this need to belong and wrestles with balancing his personal and social selves, you can provide an invaluable framework. Your family, your home life, your child's bedroom—these are domains that also deliver that sense of belonging that your child craves. As a parent you can override, at least now and then, the chorus. While helping your child find that sense of belonging, you can also balance the urge. Belonging counts, but so does personal acceptance. A child needs both.

Things You Can Do

Validate your child's need to belong.

Help your child develop an overview and an objective view of cliques.

Give your child standards to use in judging herself and others.

Suggest ways for your child to build up his self-esteem by connecting with others.

Things You Cannot Do

Give your child that sense of belonging.
Engineer your middler's place on the social ladder.
Prevent others from judging your child.
Overhaul his self-esteem for him.

STEP TWO

Help Your Child Control Emotions

Early adolescence produces a tidal wave of emotions. Young people feel frightened, overwhelmed, powerless, and in danger of being swept away. The ebb and flow of moods are often caused by the raging hormones that are part and parcel of puberty. But other forces are also involved. The social storms, which buffet many children even in the lower grades, gather force in middle school. When a child is excluded from a peer group, his feelings may run the gamut from anger to frustration to sadness.

Don't worry—you can help him gain control over his emotions. In this chapter, we will give you the tools you need to accomplish that goal. We will help you:

- Construct a "feelings" dictionary that describes your child's moods.
- Create a dialogue to encourage your child to articulate his feelings.
- Construct an action plan of positive ways to deal with each emotion.
- Cast a future strategy to anticipate and head off destructive feelings.

While we will concentrate on feelings in early adolescence, keep in mind that feelings are universal. You experience the same moods your child does. As an adult, you may have learned not to let your feelings sabotage you on the job or in your personal relationships. If not, then perhaps helping your child will also help you. You might even make this project a joint one, working on your own issues while you assist your son or daughter.

Feelings: At the Root of Friendships

There are several reasons why feelings are so important in the care and feeding of friendships.

1. *A child who can manage feelings will form more meaningful, lasting friendships.* In order for a relationship to thrive, there must be an emotional bond between the parties. Sometimes friendships falter because the initial attraction was based on the superficial—the color of someone's hair

or the clothes she was wearing—instead of deeper, more substantive characteristics such as the child's sense of humor or his empathy for others. You can help your child avoid snap judgments that could spell trouble later on.

2. *A child who can manage "bad" feelings—anger, hatred, anxiety—won't alienate those who might be friends.* If your child lashes out in anger, always appears anxious, or walks around under a cloud, she will drive away would-be friends. You want your child to see herself as others see her and have the courage to make changes. In short, you want her to be the friend she wants to have.

3. *A child who can manage feelings will have high self-esteem and be able to better weather the tricky waters of cliques.* A child who feels good about herself will recognize that emotional intelligence is not bestowed by others; it comes from within.

4. *A child who can read the emotions of others will also be able to deliver the appropriate responses and be someone who is sought out, not avoided, as a friend.* Empathy goes a long way in solidifying the bonds of friendship. Some children are not adept at reading social cues and may need parental guidance to develop this useful skill.

If you have doubts that feelings are affecting your child's friendships, listen to the following mother's plea.

"My fourteen-year-old son has a friend whose *dark moods* and *deep anger* often surface when he belittles my son. My son is easily manipulated and has *little self-confidence.* He clings to this boy because he *fears* he won't make any other friends. But this so-called friend often makes him feel *guilty* to such an extent that my son *cries.* I know this boy's parents moved from another town because of his *emotional problems.* Now I feel he is using my son to make himself look good in front of the other boys. How do I deal with my son's *anger* towards me for trying to break up this friendship and help him deal with this friend's *moods* in a confident manner, hopefully, so he can leave this boy behind?"

Every aspect of her son's interaction with his domineering peer drips with emotion. Because her son is unable to deal honestly with his own feelings, which include irrational fears that have eroded his self-esteem, he becomes the perfect victim. And the bully, battling his own emotional demons, will find no relief from his anger. Neither boy receives anything positive from this friendship.

If you have often felt like this mother, wishing that you could permanently squelch a bad friendship or protect your child from being hurt emotionally by cliques, this chapter is for you. You will learn that you can no longer pick your child's friends. What you can do is give your child the ability to name his emotions, deal with them, and use them in a positive way to manage his friendships.

Getting in Touch with Feelings

"Children first need to become aware of their own feelings so they can understand and manage them," said Phillip Mountrose in his book, *Tips and Tools for Getting Through to Kids.* "This self-awareness will bring confidence and self-esteem. It will help them connect with their experiences and be sensitive to how others feel."

You might be wondering, "Why do I need to help my child name his feelings? How can he not know what he is feeling? Doesn't he know when he is sad? Angry? Happy? Lonely?"

Not necessarily. Feelings are complex. A child may be feeling multiple emotions, a hodgepodge that leaves him confused and upset. Feelings, too, are ephemeral. They can come and go before a child can put a finger on them. Your child may not have a quick answer to the question, "What happened that makes me feel so bad?"

For some children, feelings do not come readily to the surface. Bombarded by the media, many young people have become desensitized. Movies that glorify violence have created a numbness to anger, fear, and sadness. Our fast-moving society, focused on instant gratification, has eliminated feelings of longing and anticipation that used to be common in childhood. Fantasizing about the first ride on a new bike or going to Disney World for the first time has been short-circuited, so much so that in many cases any pleasure received is short-lived. As a result, when feelings come, they hit hard. A child who has never learned to deal with disappointment and anger will find herself ill-equipped to cope.

When talking about feelings, we tend to categorize them as "bad" or "good." In fact, all emotions are simply real and tell us something about ourselves. Some "bad" feelings actually enrich our lives and give us a deeper understanding of the human experience. For example, fear may protect us in times of danger. When we are afraid, our bodies actually undergo physical changes. The adrenaline flows, our senses are heightened, and we gain newfound strength.

Even anger, perhaps the one feeling that has received the worst press, blamed for everything from child abuse to road rage to school shootings, is still a true emotion that deserves our attention and respect. Anger isn't the culprit. Rather, our response to anger is what gets us into trouble. It gets our children into trouble, too. For that reason, we will spend part of this chapter as well as part of the chapter on bullies discussing anger and giving ways to help our children channel those volatile feelings in a positive way.

In his book, *Raising an Emotionally Intelligent Child*, psychology professor John M. Gottman found that parents who practiced "emotion coaching" regarded feelings as a way to teach children about themselves and relationships. According to Gottman, those who fell down on the job made three critical mistakes:

1. *They dismissed a child's feelings.* Doing so will leave a child feeling confused. "I know I'm sad. Why does mom say I'm not?"

2. *They criticized or punished a child for his feelings.* Many boys have received the admonition, "Stop crying. Be a man." What boys learn is to suppress their emotions, something that will prove damaging not only in childhood but also in adulthood.

3. *They neglected to establish limits on negative behaviors.*

While no feelings are "bad," some behaviors are. Parents therefore still need to set limits.

We would add a number four to this list:

4. *They responded with an inappropriate emotion.* A parent may run out of patience with a child and lash out in harmful ways. For example, if your child is sad, you may get angry and try to jolt him into being happy. What happens instead, however, is that the child will be afraid to show his moods, knowing that the parent's response won't be helpful.

"Sometimes a parent is reluctant to help the child put his distress into words because he doesn't want to focus on the negative," said Elizabeth Berger, M.D., in her book, *Raising Children with Character: Parents, Trust, and the Development of Personal Integrity*. Yet without this emotional checklist, a child will be driven by his emotions and never learn to control them. Such a child will not learn to reflect beforehand on the consequences of his actions. He will react impulsively, even destructively.

One of the greatest lessons for dealing with feelings was handed out in the best-selling book *Tuesdays with Morrie*, the story of a young man who spent several months paying weekly visits to his dying college professor. Morrie advised his student, Mitch, to first let a feeling penetrate him. Whether the feeling was anger, envy, grief, or another feeling, bathe in it, wallow in it, experience it fully. Then, Morrie said, detach from it.

Feelings are real. Help your child learn what they are,

never to run away from feelings or experiences, but learn from them, then finally let them go.

Boys Are from Mars, Girls Are from Venus

Keep in mind that boys and girls deal with emotions in different ways. Many experts believe that there are actual physiological reasons for these differences. One theory says that females are better able to use both the left and right sides of their brains, thus increasing their skill for verbal and emotional expressions.

Also, as Mountrose pointed out, female and male hormones dictate how we handle feelings. "The estrogen/progesterone hormones cause females to cycle up and down with their moods; the male testosterone hormone drives boys more aggressively, focusing on efficient and quick solutions," he said.

Yet some of the ways that boys and girls react to emotions have been drilled into them by our culture. Boys are expected to be tough and not cry. Girls are seen as more emotional and therefore, it's okay for them to shed tears. Despite the women's movement and Iron John, many of us still accept and perpetuate these stereotypes with our own children. As you help your child deal with his feelings, be aware of these gender stereotypes and how they may be affecting your reactions. Talk with your parenting partner so that you are both on the same page. It's important that all children, regardless of gender, feel free to express their feelings openly.

The Name Game—
Constructing a "Feelings" Dictionary

In order to help our children name their feelings, we first need to develop our own list of words that describe a wide range of emotions. These words are necessary because our children are word-challenged when it comes to articulating their moods. We want to avoid labeling feelings "good" or "bad," so we have instead chosen the descriptive terms "up" and "down." This list, of course, is just a suggestion, but it will serve as a starting point. As you review the words, try to visualize instances where you have seen your child exhibit these emotions. Would you have been able to handle the situation better if you had been armed with these words?

Up Feelings

Happy
Accepted
Peaceful
Joyful
Contented
Energetic
Rested
Confident
Love
Excited
Proud
Calm

Down Feelings

Angry
Sad
Frustrated
Afraid
Rejected
Lethargic
Exhausted
Insecure
Hatred
Embarrassed
Guilty
Tense
Ashamed

This list will prove to be a powerful tool that you can use to take your child's emotional temperature. Don't be discouraged, however, if your child fails to respond when you run some of these words by him. It may take more than one word to draw him out.

Talk the Talk: Create a "Feelings" Dialogue

Sometimes getting a reluctant child to talk is more frustrating than trying to open a can with your bare hands. Your efforts seem futile and the more you try, the more fruitless your efforts become.

But don't give up. If your child is showing an emotion (or, the flip side, seems to be emotionless in a way that you know isn't healthy), then you need to ask, "Can we talk?"

As a first step, drop whatever you are doing and give your child your full attention. If you are on the phone, hang up. If a friend is visiting, gently show her the door. Your child needs and deserves to have you focus on him and nothing else.

Keep your body language non-threatening. Don't cross your arms or, if you are standing, don't assume a combat stance with feet apart. Close the space between yourself and your child. If your child's emotions are having a physical effect, say she is crying hysterically or he is hopping around in anger, calm the child as best you can. Get him to sit down. Maintain eye contact and establish whatever physical contact seems appropriate, from a gentle hand on a knee to an arm around his shoulders.

If your child begins to talk on his own, then listen without reacting. This may be difficult if you are upset by what you hear. Perhaps your child wasn't invited to a sleep-over birthday party. Your impulse may be to get angry, jump up, and call the offending child's parent. Hold your feelings in check. Remember, you are trying to help your child deal with her emotions. Interjecting your own feelings into the discussion will confuse her. She will no longer own the problem. And if the problem is now yours, she will see no reason to manage her feelings and work towards a solution.

When you are faced with a child who is obviously upset but can't or won't talk, you need to say something to get the conversation flowing. Here is one example of how a conversation might unfold between Jenny and her mother. Jenny comes home from school and, without taking her coat off, grabs a soda out of the refrigerator and heads upstairs. Jenny's mother has just gotten home from work and has begun preparing dinner, but she senses that something is not right with her daughter. She could let it go. After all, Jenny didn't seek her out and dinner will be late if things don't get into the oven. But Jenny's mother knows she needs to check on her daughter.

She taps on Jenny's door and finds her daughter lying on her bed staring at the ceiling.

MOTHER: "Hi. Do you have a minute?"

Jenny doesn't respond, so her mother comes in and sits on the bed beside Jenny. She lightly places her hand on Jenny's leg.

MOTHER: "I can see that you are pretty upset."

Again, Jenny doesn't respond.

MOTHER: "Would it help to talk?"

Jenny shrugs.

MOTHER: "Well, remember the other day when I lost that big account at work?"

Jenny nods.

MOTHER: "I was pretty angry. But when I got home, you asked me what was wrong, and after talking about it, I was able to let go of my anger. I should have had that account, but now I see there were some things I could have done to really sew up the deal. If I had stayed angry, I wouldn't have been able to look at the situation objectively. You helped me out, Jen. Can I return the favor?"

By this time, Jenny is softening. Using herself as an example, her mother has aligned herself with her daughter. In her short statement, she also accomplished several other important things. She named her own feeling—anger—and pointed out that without Jenny's intervention she might have taken longer to work through her problem. Once she was able to let go of the anger, she was once again in control.

JENNY: "Well, Katie has tickets to a concert this weekend that every girl in school wants to go to. Her father told her she could invite two friends and she chose Marisa and Ashley, not me."

MOTHER: "You really wanted to go to the concert."

JENNY: "More than anything! I'll die if I can't go!"

MOTHER: "So I guess you're pretty angry at Katie."

JENNY: "Really angry! I mean, how could she invite Marisa and Ashley? She's known me longer."

MOTHER: "It's true you've known Katie since kindergarten, but I didn't think you've been as close to her this year."

JENNY: "It's not my fault! Debbie and Alison don't like Katie and won't eat lunch with me if I sit with her."

MOTHER: "So you had to choose between your friends. How did that make you feel? Guilty for leaving Katie behind?"

JENNY: "Really guilty. Katie and I had always been so close. I thought she would understand."

MOTHER: "Perhaps she was hurt when you chose Debbie and Alison over her."

Jenny nods.

MOTHER: "Well, so perhaps you are feeling a little sad that you have lost Katie as a friend?"

Jenny nods again.

MOTHER: "So what do you think you could do to get things back on track?"

JENNY: "Talk to Katie tomorrow at school about how awful I feel about the way I treated her."

MOTHER: "It's still too late to get an invitation to the concert."

JENNY: "I don't care about that anymore. But I do care about losing Katie as a friend."

By continuing to gently probe and offer Jenny words from the "feelings" dictionary, her mother was able to help her separate and deal with several emotions. Sure, Jenny was angry she wasn't invited to the concert. But she was also feeling guilty about abandoning Katie and sad that she had lost her childhood friend. Also, by getting in touch with her own feelings, Jenny was able to understand what her friend Katie was feeling. Once Jenny could understand where her emotion was coming from, she was able to come up with an action plan—to apologize to Katie and try to restore the friendship. Without her mother's intervention, Jenny might have been stuck in her anger.

Walk the Walk—Construct an Action Plan

Of course, Jenny's mother was lucky in that she hit the right note and got her daughter to open up. But sometimes adolescents are immutable, refusing to talk. What do you do if you are faced with that situation?

One alternative is to keep the door open. "I know you don't feel like talking now. But if you change your mind, maybe we can talk later." Watch for a moment when your child seems relaxed and may be coaxed into talking. In surveys we did for *The Roller-Coaster Years*, parents told us that bedtime and driving in the car were two times when their children were most loquacious; bedtime, because the sleepy child oftentimes becomes the talkative child, and driving in the car because you are in an enclosed space with your child, no interruptions, both strapped in facing forward. A mobile confessional.

As Jenny's mother did, use "I" statements that avoid questions, such as "I see that you are very quiet and may be thinking about something serious."

Another idea is to encourage the child to work through the situation on her own. "I can see that you are so upset you can't talk. Why don't you try writing a letter to Katie to tell her how you feel? You don't have to mail it. But getting your thoughts down on paper may help you understand what you are feeling."

Journal-writing is very popular among teenagers these days. If your child keeps one, encourage her to take it out and write. Being able to express feelings, whether verbally or on paper, can move a child entrenched in anger and sadness towards a resolution. If your child needs help getting started, you can make some suggestions. For example, "I know you're angry that Josh was chosen for the soccer team and you weren't. Why don't you write in your journal about how you are feeling? What would you say to the coach? How about Josh? Will it be hard to be friends with him still?"

Your son may not respond, but hopefully he will take pen to paper and pour some of his emotions out onto the page. Journaling will aid him in dealing with his anger and disappointment, and help him confront his relationships with the coach and Josh.

Another exercise is to suggest your child merely write down adjectives and phrases that describe what he is feeling. The young boy above might compose a list that includes: "angry, mad, jealous, sad, slow, clumsy, bad kicker, could have done better, shouldn't have missed practice." So, in a short list, he has moved from being angry to seeing that perhaps he caused the problem by not practicing enough.

The latter is important because there's always a next time. And that's the valuable lesson we want our children to take away with them. We want our children to know that in some cases—not all—the choices we make dictate the outcome. Children who consistently make bad choices suffer. Children who learn from their mistakes by paying attention to their feelings thrive. The down feelings are eventually replaced with up feelings. "Things didn't go so well this time and now I'm feeling bad. How can I make sure things go better next time?" For Jenny, it might mean choosing her friends with more care. For the soccer player, practice, practice, practice.

Anger—Using It and Controlling It

Here's a true story. One day on a quiet street on Long Island, New York, two boys, ages nine and thirteen, were comparing their collections of Pokémon cards. The nine-year-old became angry because he thought the older boy had taken his Hitmonlee, one of the more difficult cards to acquire. An argument ensued and the nine-year-old stabbed his friend. He was later charged with second-degree assault.

Was the nine-year-old's anger justified? Yes.

Was his reaction? Of course not.

It's okay to be angry. It's not okay to be angry and verbally or physically abuse another person. That lesson is difficult enough for many adults to master. For children, particularly for adolescent boys out to prove their manhood, it is particularly challenging. Because friendships are so volatile in middle school, anger is a frequent companion. But a child who is always angry with no mechanism to work through those feelings will alienate others and condemn himself to a lifetime of stressful, unfulfilling relationships. Helping our children understand and deal with anger is perhaps one of the greatest lessons we can teach them.

Anger is an important feeling that should not be dismissed. At its most primitive level, it signals us that our needs are not being met. That lack of gratification may be our own fault. The young soccer player we cited earlier, for example, was at fault for not practicing more. But too often, a child will be tempted to blame his anger on someone else. "It's the coach's fault." If we allow a child to get away with this reasoning, he risks casting himself as a victim, a role that will lead to problems, even disaster.

That's what happened in Columbine, Colorado, to Dylan Klebold and Eric Harris. The two teenagers were angry that they had been shunned by other students at the school. They saw themselves as victims and vowed to get even. They did, going on a shooting rampage that killed twelve students and one teacher.

Of course, not all angry adolescents erupt in such violent ways. Many lash out verbally at parents, teachers, and friends. Others who internalize the anger may channel it into destructive behavior, using sex, alcohol, drugs, or an eating disorder to numb their pain. None of these routes will lead to success, particularly where friendships are concerned, so it's imperative for parents to show their children how to use, not abuse, their anger.

How is that done? We recommend these steps:

1. *Identify hot buttons.* Some people get angry when they encounter a rude salesperson. What sets your child off? Are there certain children, situations, or names that always push his buttons? Have him write these things down so he can be on guard.

2. *Observe the warning signs.* Anger builds before it erupts. Teach your child to recognize his personal warning

signs. These may include: feeling hot and sweating, clenching his fists, rapid breathing, and losing focus.

3. *Visualize the anger.* Help your child see his anger as either a balloon about to burst, a boiling pot of water, a stick of dynamite, or a volcano. Stress that he is in control and can effect the outcome, he can let out the air, turn down the heat, and prevent an explosion.

4. *Release the energy.* Anger produces newfound energy. Teach your child to stay calm by taking deep breaths and counting. Often this means walking away from a confrontation until he can cool down and think more clearly.

5. *Express anger in words.* To get to the source of his anger, show your child that it is proper for him to explain to another person why he got angry. In doing so, he should use "I" statements. "I get angry when you criticize me on the soccer field in front of the other players." As an alternative, he could write a letter to the person who made him angry, even if he doesn't plan to deliver it.

6. *Detach from the source of anger.* Oftentimes your child will have no control over the person or event that is sparking his anger. A troublesome classmate who is bent on annoying him may not stop his teasing. In this case, your child has to make the decision to reject his peer's comments and not react. This is a tough lesson for young adolescents who are so sensitive to their public image. But chances are the antagonist is looking for a reaction. If your child produces none, he will move on to other victims.

Anger is caused by hurt feelings and a loss of control. No group feels less in control than middlers. They may get angry when ordered around by parents and teachers. And they get angry when they can't control their friendships. We can't control their friendships, either. But we can help them deal with the anger that these liaisons may produce.

Roadblocks to Friendships—
Fear, Sadness, Shyness

In our survey for *The Roller-Coaster Years*, we asked adolescents to name their biggest fears. Number one on the list was social anxiety. "I worry about everyone hating me," said one fourteen-year-old girl.

In some cases, adolescents become their own worst enemies in the battle to make and keep friends. Worry about being accepted can trigger feelings that actually stand in the way of friendships. A child who is afraid to approach others, too shy to start a conversation, and who appears sad because of her social state will not be sought after by others.

Actresses who play teenagers in the TV show *Popular* were asked by *Jump* magazine to reflect on their own social struggles when they were in school. "Everyone is so worried about trying to fit in, and it's scary to stand out and be different—to be yourself," said Leslie Bibb, who plays blonde Brooke McQueen on the show.

We can help our children by pointing out that how we think governs how we feel. If we can put our thought process to work, we can shift our moods. Take fear, for example. Ask your child to write down what she is afraid of. Tell her to be specific. Saying, "no one likes me," is too general. One entry on her list might be: "I'm afraid no one will talk to me at the dance." You can then talk with her about who will be there that she might approach to talk. You might even role play with her to come up with opening lines. "Isn't this music great? I would love to get this CD."

Adolescents who appear shy may be afraid to take risks socially. Another *Popular* actress acknowledged this fact. "The thing is, I thought that by keeping to myself I was cool, but actually, it was just a defense mechanism," said Sara Rue, who plays Carmen Ferrara. "I didn't give people the choice of liking me or not liking me. I just decided that they wouldn't and then never talked to them."

Parents need to remind their children to be the friend they want to have. Adolescents are attracted to those who are interesting, appear confident, and are comfortable with themselves. Leslie Grossman, who plays preppie Mary Cherry on *Popular*, observed: "I think if you're feeling alienated or freaked out, which I know everyone does at some point, you should do something really positive. If you're good at the guitar, play guitar. Or dance, be in a play, write in your journal—anything. Do something that's yours and that nobody else can judge, because when you're feeling your worst, that's when you get to know yourself best."

Green-Eyed Monsters: Hatred and Jealousy

Like all feelings, hatred and jealousy tell us more about ourselves than they do about others. When we are jealous of someone else it means that we are not feeling good about ourselves and need to work on self-esteem. Hatred signals that we have very strong feelings for someone. And whether those feelings are justified or not, we need to probe further. It may mean that we have some unresolved business we need to get off our agenda. Talking with the other person may be in order.

When you sense that your daughter harbors jealousy or hatred towards a classmate, you shouldn't dismiss her words. Again, her feelings are telling you something that deserves your full attention. Her self-esteem is hurting and she needs to find out why.

First, validate her feelings. Jealousy and hatred are universal feelings that we have all shared at one time or another. You might even mention some of your own struggles trying to conquer these monsters.

Suggest that she write down why she has these feelings towards the other person. Just seeing her reasons in print may convince her they are irrational. For example, being jealous of another girl because her hair always looks great will seem frivolous. If her feelings are more justified—perhaps she dislikes someone who has hurt her in some way—encourage her to talk with this person. If that's not possible, help her to understand that she is letting this person have control over her. Suggest she try to get rid of the hatred by writing this person a letter and then tearing it up.

Shame and Guilt: Two Emotions That Erode the Spirit

These two emotions are cousins—related but separate. Shame is something a child feels because of who he is. That may be due to a home situation that is not of his making. Shame may also result when something is done to the child. Sexual abuse, for example, leaves its victims feeling shameful.

Guilt, on the other hand, usually results when a child does something wrong and then feels badly about it. This situation is by far the easier one for a parent to tackle. You can suggest definite steps, such as an apology, restitution, or a punishment, that will wipe the slate clean.

A child who feels shame will be more difficult to handle and may need professional help. You can encourage the child to counter the bad feelings by listing the good qualities about himself. You can also encourage him to detach from the shame in his life. If his father is an alcoholic, for example, you can point out that the problem is his father's, not his.

Feelings and Substance Abuse

Adolescents who are overwhelmed with their feelings may turn to alcohol or drugs for a solution. When an adolescent is feeling bad, drugs or alcohol can alleviate the pain and make him feel better. However, in the long run, this alternative will be destructive to the child's future. He will not learn how to handle his feelings, and he may very well harm himself, or kill himself, before he has the chance.

Be aware that substance abuse changes the way a child acts. Parents should do everything possible to stay emotionally connected to their children so they can detect mood swings that may be caused by alcohol or drugs. You may notice that your child's emotions swing widely depending upon what he is using when. You should seek the help of a professional immediately. (For more information, refer to our chapter on alcohol and drugs in *Parenting 911.)*

Feelings and Friendships

Learning to handle our feelings, unfortunately, is not something that comes automatically with maturity. How many of us know adults who are never in control of their emotions? Adolescence is a prime time for focusing on moods because feelings play such a large role in how our children form and keep friendships. We need to deal with the "down" emotions even more than the "up" emotions because these are the ones that hurt relationships.

A child who learns to control his feelings will feel better about himself and enjoy better relationships with everyone in his life. "Only very slowly does the child begin to understand in a sustained way that other people are truly entitled to feel things, to believe things, and to want things that are different from his own feelings, beliefs, and desires," said Gary Egeberg in his book, *My Feelings Are Like Wild Ani-*

mals. And that, in essence, is one of the tenets of true friendship.

Things You Can Do

Voice your own feelings loudly and often.

Use your "feelings" dictionary to help your child name his feelings.

Gently probe by using "I" statements to encourage dialogue.

Suggest writing exercises so your child can work out her feelings.

Listen without being judgmental.

Have your child record his moods, what triggered them, what he wanted to do, what he did to get out of the mood.

Have your child draw a picture or sketch his feelings.

Things You Cannot Do

Take away the "bad" feelings.

Change your child's mood.

Dictate how your child should feel.

Change how others feel about your child.

STEP THREE

Disarm Your Bully

If popularity in school is a game, then some children win by stacking the deck. They control the cards, they control who is dealt a winning or a losing hand. They envision themselves as the kings and queens of the social parade and they work hard to surround themselves with the jacks and the aces who will back them up when the chips are down. The losers? These are the children who become the class jokers, sentenced to a school lifetime of torment.

If you are parenting one of these kings or queens, you may feel like you have hit the jackpot. After all, you want your child to be popular, to be sought after by peers, to be viewed as a born leader. But, be careful. Your child may not be a benevolent despot. He may have more in common with Attila the Hun, and she with Lady Macbeth.

Bullying has reached epidemic proportions in our schools and current trends contradict our previous perceptions. First of all, bullies are no longer just boys. Girls have now proven that they can be every bit as cruel as their male counterparts. The bully is no longer the outsider, the rebel, the most unpopular kid in class. Rather, he may be an honor student or the captain of the soccer team. She may be the head cheerleader or president of the class.

Perhaps the biggest change has been that the bully no longer acts alone. Rather, he or she operates in a clique. Even in bullying, it seems, there is safety, and more power, in numbers.

All parents need to be concerned about bullies. Subsequent chapters will deal with the victims, those who are targeted, and the bystanders, those who watch but don't get involved. Here, though, we will deal with the actual bullies—the leaders and the followers. In this chapter we will help you:

- Understand how bullies manipulate peers through cliques.
- Objectively evaluate your child's behavior.
- Develop a vocabulary to discuss your concerns with your child.
- Begin behavior modification exercises with your child.

Like most parents, you are probably ready to defend your child against charges that he is a bully leader or follower. "He's only taking care of himself," you might say. Going to middle school can be a bit like running the gauntlet. Children spend their days dodging the emotional slings and arrows that have the power to inflict deep psychological scars. You want your child to avoid being hit. But you also must be concerned that he is not the one hurting others. Why? Hopefully, you will want to do so to create a kinder and gentler school environment. But if you can't think in such philanthropic terms, at least consider this: In the new school order, victims are fighting back. When they do, they retaliate, and sometimes kill, those who have harmed them. What goes around, comes around. You need to stop that cycle.

Bullies—Damaging Themselves and Others

Any parent who suspects his child of bullying behavior would do well to address the problem sooner rather than later.

1. *Bullies don't burn out; they get older.* And they maintain that bully-like behavior throughout life. A child who bullies his classmates will turn into a young adult who harasses his girlfriend, a husband who abuses his wife, a father who beats his children, and a boss who torments his employees.

2. *Bullies often become criminals.* Child bullies often have problems as adults. One study showed that by age thirty, 25% of adults who had been identified as bullies as children

had racked up criminal records, as opposed to 5% of those who hadn't been bullies.

3. *Bullies affect a large group of schoolchildren.* According to the National Association of School Psychologists (NASP), about one in seven schoolchildren is a bully or victim. The problem affects about 5 million elementary and middle school students in the U.S. For fourth through eighth graders, 22% report academic difficulties resulting from peer abuse.

Bullying, 2000 Style

What is bullying?

Bullying is when one or several students employ physical, emotional, or verbal abuse to make life miserable for another student. In most cases, the victim has done nothing deliberate to invite such negative attention. He may stand out because he looks or acts differently (see the following chapter on victims).

The abuse can take many forms, from simple name-calling to physical abuse to sexual harassment. What defines the torment as bullying is its intensity and duration. "What distinguishes [a bully] from someone who teases occasionally is a pattern of *repeated* physical or psychological intimidation," said Allan L. Beane in his book, *The Bully Free Classroom*. In the world of the victim, "Nowhere to run, Nowhere to hide," could be the theme song. It's no surprise then that according to a report from the NASP, one hundred sixty thousand students stay home from school each day because they are afraid of being targeted for such abuse.

Bullying has been around for a long time. Way back in 1850, Thomas Hughes wrote *Tom Brown's Schooldays* and described various tortures the title character was forced to endure at the hands of his classmates. And would Oliver Twist, in Charles Dickens's classic tale, have asked, "Please sir, I want some more," unless he had been threatened by the bullies at the orphanage?

Today, more children take their cues from TV, movies, and music videos than from books. There is now a formidable mass of research showing that children who watch violent media behave more aggressively. (The *Harvard Mental Health Letter* cites more than fifty field studies over the last twenty years that have found this link.) Just as impressive are the many anecdotes brought to us by those who visit our message boards on "Parent Soup." This is what one thirteen-year-old girl told us: "I saw a movie that had vulgar language. Later on, I was angry at my dad and used a vulgarity to describe him to my mom. Well, she never said anything. But a few seconds afterward I was shocked at what the movie had done to my speech!"

Out of the mouths of babes! This thirteen-year-old was savvy enough to realize what had happened and correct her behavior. But for many young adolescents, life begins to imitate art. What they see on TV and in the movies gives them a blueprint for how to act within their peer group. Much of what they watch reinforces the power of the bully. Shows like *Beverly Hills 90210* and *Popular,* as well as movies like *She's All That* and *I Know What You Did Last Summer*, have made bullying chic. In these electronic versions, bullies look like Sarah Michelle Gellar or Ryan Philippe, who co-starred in *Cruel Intentions*, a *Dangerous Liaisons* for the teen set. In these media events, the bullies are not the class weirdos or loners, but instead have good looks, money, smarts, and plenty of friends. How they keep those friends, however, gets to the heart of their bullying behavior. They acquire their friends through threats and intimidation rather than through honesty and loyalty. But many young adolescents, particularly those who are worried about maintaining friendships, don't focus on the means, only the results. They see that bullies occupy the power center. The temptation to emulate these power-brokers is irresistible.

A Primer on Bullying

There are many different forms of bullying. In order for you to "talk the talk" with your son or daughter, you should educate yourself on how the process works now. Many of these tactics follow along gender lines, with girls exerting more psychological control and boys, more physical control.

HOW GIRLS BULLY

If you have a daughter, then you know how emotional her friendships can become. Young adolescent girls pour their hearts and souls into their relationships. When those liaisons go sour—this happens weekly, daily, even hourly in middle school—the psychological ramifications can be brutal.

Bullies quickly seize on the idea of using friendship as a weapon in the clique battle. Here are the tactics that are most commonly employed:

1. *Scapegoating.* A member of the clique or an outside girl is targeted for abuse. Girls receive their marching orders: "Don't talk to Jennifer. Marcy (the clique leader) is angry at her." Why? A reason may not be given. If Jennifer has been a member of the clique, she may have been challenging Marcy's authority. In order to reestablish her power and put Jennifer in her place, Marcy initiates the scapegoating. If Jennifer is an outside girl, the reasons for targeting her may be irrational. Perhaps she is new to the school, a member of a minority—she could even be the prettiest girl in the school.

What happens? Everyone stops talking to Jennifer. She's the last one selected for a team in gym. No one will share a microscope with her in biology. She eats her lunch alone. Dirty looks, snide comments, pushes and shoves may add to Jennifer's humiliation. By the end of the day, she will be distraught, in tears, unsure what she did to cause such ill-treatment. The truth is probably that she didn't do anything.

2. *Backstabbing.* How best to get back at someone than to reveal a secret? When Jennifer and Marcy were friends, Jennifer confided to her that she had once made an anonymous phone call to Stephanie, calling her fat. Now Marcy

sets out to use that information as ammunition in her war against Jennifer. She manages to sit next to Stephanie at lunch and reveal Jennifer's secret. Stephanie, who up until now has remained neutral to Jennifer, is justifiably angry and enlists in Marcy's army. Stephanie's other friends follow suit. Now, Jennifer is truly out in the cold. And when one of the girls mentions the phone call to a teacher, Jennifer finds that not even the adults will sympathize with her plight.

At home, Jennifer is ashamed to tell her parents what is happening to her. After supper, she hides in her room. She goes on-line for a while, but quickly signs off when she begins receiving nasty e-mails from classmates, chastising her for her remarks against Stephanie. She dreads going to school the next day.

3. *Belittling.* Jennifer is not even in the door before the attack begins. Belittling, face-to-face verbal assaults delivered with a smile, a smirk, or in a note, continue throughout the day. "Are you auditioning to become a clown with all that makeup?" or, "Whatever were you thinking when you got dressed this morning?" and, of course, "Made any anonymous phone calls lately?"

4. *Rumors.* Marcy is not through yet. Next she will employ the grapevine, deliberately passing along a juicy tidbit about Jennifer. The rumor isn't true, but no one cares. If you think what we're describing is fiction, here's the real-life version we heard on-line from one mother: "My thirteen-year-old daughter's friend spread lies, telling everyone at school that my daughter is pregnant. My poor child is so

hurt and feels betrayed by this girl. I've talked to my child but cannot calm her down. She's forbidden me to confront her accuser or talk to this girl's parents about this slander." As you can see, the rumors are typically sexual in nature. Themes of being pregnant, promiscuous, engaging in oral sex, or being gay are the most typical.

The Internet has helped to fuel the rumor mill. With e-mail, the rumor-monger can easily send the false missive to dozens of students. Often, the person spreading the lies can hide her identity in cyberspace, thus making it difficult, if not impossible, to trace the source.

By this point, Jennifer has been through the middle school chamber of horrors. After three days of enduring the cold shoulder, nasty remarks, and salacious rumors, she is rightly devastated. She has headaches and stomachaches. She can't eat. Soon, her marks will start to plummet and even the things she enjoyed doing—sports, music, going to the movies—hold no appeal. Every social event is another occasion for her to be humiliated. She may begin to hate herself, too, and it's only a short step until she starts using drugs, alcohol, or self-mutilation to ease her pain.

What are the other girls feeling about the situation? Marcy, the ringleader, is feeling powerful. She may even feel justified in what she has done. After all, Jennifer did make that nasty call to Stephanie. Didn't she deserve to suffer because of that? That the crime hardly fit the punishment (to say nothing of the fact that Marcy shouldn't have been the one to do the punishing) doesn't enter her thinking.

The other girls in the clique are now ambivalent. On one

hand, they are pumped up because they backed their leader and stuck together. A nagging voice in each girl's head, however, chants: "Will you be next?"

Can things get worse? Actually, they can. Unless Marcy calls off her troops, Jennifer could be subjected to a direct physical assault. If you think girls don't go postal, think again. Although girls are not as violent as boys, one harbinger of the trend was uncovered recently in a study among girls in a Philadelphia middle school. The researchers found that 65% of the girls engaged in some form of physical aggression such as pushing or shoving directed at boys. Only 43% of boys, on the other hand, admitted to violent behavior against girls. Young adolescent females getting physical signals trouble ahead. Whatever happened to the girls who just wanted to have fun?

HOW BOYS BULLY

If you have a son you know that, compared to girls, male friendships turn less on emotions and more on action. Boys, for the most part, don't spend their time confiding in each other. They find it hard to play "I've Got a Secret," using confidences to torture someone. However, most male bullies still have a variety of methods that can be used to turn a classmate into a victim:

1. *Broadcasting strengths.* A bully assembles a posse by playing up his strengths and hiding his weaknesses. Take the case of Justin, for example. Justin doesn't do that well in the classroom, but he excels on the playing fields. He takes

advantage of that, using his athletic prowess as a way of attracting friends. Other boys want to be with him, not only because he is a good soccer player, but also because that status wins him the admiration of girls. Given the right circumstances, a boy like Justin could develop into a true leader. On the other hand, he can just as easily become a bully, attempting to preserve his position by humiliating others.

2. *Rumors.* Like girls, boys employ the rumor mill. This turns out to be a favorite tool for a bully like Justin. Another boy on the soccer team, Evan, has been Justin's rival ever since they hit middle school. Evan does well academically, but he is also a good athlete. Unfortunately, he is shy and has never had many friends. Justin decides to target him and begins by spreading the rumor that Evan is a "faggot" or "gay." The ploy is effective because anyone who defends Evan risks being tagged gay, too. Among adolescent boys, who are just beginning to define themselves sexually, being called homosexual is frightening.

In Evan's case, the rumor isn't true, but that doesn't matter. Once the rumor is started, everyone repeats it and soon it becomes a statement of fact. Evan unwittingly plays into Justin's hands by being too physical with the other boys during the games—slapping them on the back, hugging them after a goal, sitting too close on the bench. Because Evan has few friends, he relishes the time he spends playing soccer. That's when he feels accepted as a bona fide member of the male community. But his membership card is now in danger of being canceled by Justin and his accomplices.

3. *Fights.* Physical rumblings are part of the boy culture. One fight a year per boy is considered normal. These fights can be friendly jostles that escalate or body slamming assaults. Some are spontaneous. Others are calculated at the bus stop, in the locker room, or on the playground. In Justin's case, the fight with Evan is premeditated. The other boys, rather than telling an adult so that the fight can be averted, plan to watch (more on the role of these "innocent" bystanders in Step Five).

We heard the following lament on-line from the mother of a real-life Evan: "My eighth-grade son was punched in the face at school yesterday after football practice. I am so angry that this happened. Angry because it happened in the school building and no adult knew about it until I went into the school to get my son. How does this happen, when a volleyball game is going on not more than 100 feet away, with several teachers, school officials, etc., watching? Aren't schools supposed to be a safe place for our children?" Bullies are clever enough to stage their assaults far enough away from the adults that no one knows what's happened. None of the students who witness attacks are likely to come forward, either.

4. *Weapons.* Often the bully leader or one of his associates will be armed with more than knuckles. This eighth-grade mother we just heard from continues: "One of the bullies that was in on the fight has been bringing a pocket knife to school. My son saw it in one of the classes." Fortunately, the knife was not used in the attack on her son, but it could have been.

5. *Deliberate humiliations.* Even the fight doesn't end Justin's abuse of Evan. He looks for any opportunity to torture him and isolate him from the other students. Other members of Justin's posse willingly participate. One day, Evan is stuffed into his locker. After Evan shouts, he is finally let out by the school custodian. Each day at lunch, someone shakes Evan down for his lunch money. He begins bringing his lunch from home. That won't work, either—the other boys steal his paper sack.

Soon the humiliations become even more unbearable. One day before soccer practice, he is subjected to "pantsing," being ambushed and having his pants pulled down in front of a group of girls. In the locker room, he endures a "swirly," where he is turned upside down by his assailants and dunked into a lavatory toilet bowl.

Evan's performance on the soccer field falters. How could it not? The coach thinks he is just not working hard anymore and makes him sit out the next game. His parents, who have come to watch, are bewildered by Evan's behavior. He has become withdrawn and noncommunicative. He tells his parents he wants to drop off the team.

What about Justin? His status as soccer star has been solidified. He is feeling powerful and proud. Evan is no longer a threat to him. The other boys have rallied around Justin, although not because they admire him as a team player, but because they fear his wrath. When the soccer team loses an important game, several boys wonder what might have been if Evan had played. No one, however, is ready to step forward and challenge Justin. All the adults remain oblivious to what has happened.

Because he's a boy, Evan will try to remain stoic about his situation. It isn't manly to tattle, particularly while he is still battling rumors about his sexual orientation. His few friends have long since deserted him, afraid that they will be targeted next. *Lord of the Flies* lives.

Sexual Harassment: When Bullying Crosses the Line

Some of the bullying that Evan endured was sexual harassment. School administrators are concerned about sexual harassment for two reasons. One, it's illegal and two, it affects school safety. "School safety is more than metal detectors and see-through backpacks and getting rid of lockers," said Nan Stein, director of the Project on Bullying and Sexual Harassment in Schools at Wellesley College. "There are sexual assaults in school. There are rapes. Some kids are afraid to go to school because of sexual harassment."

Unwanted touching—grabbing a girl's breast, slapping a boy on his behind, for example—constitutes sexual harassment. There is a large gray area, however, which encompasses everything that falls short of direct physical contact. School officials have often looked the other way when the offense involved things like name-calling, passing around sexually explicit magazines, or starting sexually oriented rumors.

That said, school administrators draw the line in different places, depending upon the reading of any given situation. In one school, an adolescent boy might find himself in trouble after making just one sexually explicit comment to a girl. In another school, however, the same kind of offense might not be punished until the harassment becomes persistent and severe. Still another school might try to ignore the situation altogether (though school officials will take it seriously when the girl's parents threaten to file suit).

Most people think of sexual harassment as being one-on-one. A boy harassing a girl is the most talked about combination. These days, however, sexual harassment often becomes a group activity, another way for the clique leader to assemble the troops and wield power. An alarming trend is individual boys being targeted by a group of their peers. Groton Academy, a well-to-do boarding school in Massachusetts, was rocked in March 2000 when an eighteen-year-old boy charged that he was sexually assaulted as a freshman on his third day at the school. He told a shocked assembly that he was held down by four older boys who grabbed his genitals, licked his face, and sexually assaulted him. Soon, other boys came forward and also admitted to being sexually harassed.

What came out of the Groton controversy is that some harassment is not only tolerated but expected. Adults, particularly when the situation involves boys, look the other way. One boy at Groton was quoted as saying: "Boys grabbing each others' [testicles] is a common occurrence at Groton. It's sort of a form of greeting. Do I think it's wrong?

Yeah, but it happens all the time. In front of the teachers, in full view of everyone. And if you complain about it, well, you know, you just don't."

From your point of view, you want to make sure that your child is neither the target nor the ringleader for such sexual antics. Remember those discussions you had with your child when he was five about not letting anyone touch his "private places?" It's time to have those discussions again. Your child may know not to fondle or grope a fellow student, but does he truly understand what constitutes sexual harassment? Don't take the attitude exhibited by a mother in Larchmont, New York, whose eleven-year-old son was suspended for sexual harassment. "This is a kid who doesn't know what sex is, what harassment is," the mother told the *New York Times*, defending her position to oppose the school. Make sure your child does understand sexual harassment. Consider this example:

For a long time Dennis has had a crush on Heather. Yet aside from exchanging a word or two during history class, Heather ignores him. Her indifference has angered Dennis. Most of the boys know he likes her and have begun teasing him. To save face among his friends and to get back at Heather for putting him in this position, he begins to harass her. He begins by positioning himself near the girls' locker room each morning before school. So that his actions won't go unobserved by his friends, he invites several of them to join him. When Heather approaches, he and his friends make loud sucking noises and call out to her using derogatory language. At first Heather is so shocked, she doesn't even realize this display is aimed at her. As the day progresses and the harassment continues, she becomes acutely aware and embarrassed.

Heather also is feeling confused and guilty. Her sweater, bought last year, is tighter than she remembered. Is she inviting some of this abuse by appearing too sexy? She was aware of Dennis's interest. Had she been rude to him? Does she deserve what he is dishing out?

By the second day, the harassment has taken on a life of its own. Dennis's friends are now egging him on. Even if he wanted to stop, which he doesn't at this point, it would be hard to do so. Dennis, however, is relishing the activity. For one thing, Heather no longer ignores him. And he has certainly scored points with his friends. If he considers the situation at all from Heather's point of view, he is inclined to believe that she is enjoying all the attention. When his parents receive a call from school saying that their son is being charged with sexual harassment, no one is more surprised than Dennis.

While we have looked at a situation where a boy is harassing a girl, the sexes could easily be switched. Think of a group of girls loudly rating a boy's "butt." It happens.

Your Child: True Leader or a Bully?

Sometimes a bully's behavior is so overt, parents cannot remain ignorant. "My ten-year-old stepdaughter is the ringleader for a group of girls at her school that constantly picks on an underprivileged girl," one mother told us. "My stepdaughter makes fun of this girl because she has to wear the same pants to school almost every day and her hair is never done. This girl finally stood up to my stepdaughter and threatened to kick her. But a couple of the girls who worship my stepdaughter told the girl they would kill her if she did anything." In this situation, there's no doubt that the stepdaughter is a ringleader and her parents must deal with it.

On the other hand, you may find it hard to see your son or daughter in any of the examples we have presented so far. Keep in mind, however, that young adolescents act differently around adults than they act around their peers. That polite, considerate child you observe at home may be a manipulative ringleader in school. Remember Eddie Haskell? He behaved like the model child in front of Beaver's parents. But when left alone with his friends, his true colors came out. June Cleaver's antenna picked up on the negative signals she received from Eddie. So keep your radar on, too. Here are some ways to objectively assess your child's behavior:

1. *Listen when she talks about her friends.* Bullies often will put other children down just to make themselves look good. Does your child do that when she talks about the daily events in school? We don't advocate eavesdropping on your child, but there are times when you can be a fly on the wall. One mother told us this tale: "I drove my daughter and her friends to soccer practice the other day and was upset with the conversation. They were plotting to tease a girl in their class. Later, I told my daughter I didn't approve

of her behavior. She just laughed and said that this girl was annoying and deserved to be teased. I was horrified! How could I have raised such an insensitive child?"

2. *Watch how he treats his siblings.* Does your son tease and bully his brothers and sisters? Chances are he is dishing out the same abuse in the classroom. Bullies oftentimes cannot turn off their behavior at home.

3. *Talk to your daughter's teachers.* Most teachers have a pretty good idea who the ringleaders and followers are in each class. When you attend parent-teacher conferences, make some time to talk about the social side of middle school. Ask whether your daughter is inclusive. How does she get along with her classmates?

4. *Talk to the other parents.* Say you go to the next PTA meeting and hear that a boy in the class, Aaron, has been bullying the other kids. You know that your son has been spending a lot of time with Aaron these days. Could he be Aaron's accomplice?

5. *Monitor his media diet.* Has your son been fixated on shoot-'em-up video games or violent movies? Could he be bringing that confrontational attitude with him to school? Does your daughter spend her leisure time watching TV shows where the popular characters "dis" each other? Do you have the feeling that she admires these young people? Now is the time to make it very clear to your child how you feel about all this.

6. *Evaluate your home situation objectively.* Step back and consider how you treat your children and the adults in your

life. Is there anything in your behavior that could make your children see you as a bully? Are you setting a positive example for them or do you send the message that bullying others is the way to get ahead?

7. *Squelch the green-eyed monster.* Do you sense that your child is jealous of his peers? Does he always talk about what the other kids in his class have that he doesn't? Do you have the sneaking suspicion that he might resort to bullying tactics to get back at some of his more fortunate classmates? Are there things you are doing at home to encourage these feelings, such as always talking about what you don't have or casting your family as the have-nots and his classmates' families as the haves? Take the opportunity to talk about jealousy. There will always be people who have more. But the things that really count in life can't be bought. Don't assume he knows this.

8. *Don't try to choose your child's friends.* Are you so intent on having a popular child that you push your daughter towards those who may be a negative influence? Remember that young adolescents sometimes put on false faces for adults. That sweet, pretty, popular girl who visits your house and is always polite may, in fact, be the clique leader ready to lead your daughter down the wrong path. Your role as a parent is to talk about friendships. But trust your child to make the right choices.

9. *Assess your child's social skills.* Sometimes children resort to bullying or following a bully because they lack the ability to make true friends. This area is one where you can

act as a coach, helping your child make and keep friends (we will cover this topic in more depth in the bystander chapter).

10. *Watch for sudden signs of affluence.* Bullies often "shake down" their victims. If your son suddenly sports new sunglasses, a new jacket or hat, or comes home with an expensive portable CD player, the warning bells should go off. Unless he has used his birthday money or saved his allowance, it's possible the new possessions were not given to him voluntarily.

11. *Deny the denial.* No parent wants to be told that they are parenting a bully. But if he walks like a bully, and talks like a bully, he's probably a bully. Don't waste time justifying his behavior. Put your efforts into turning your child around.

Sensitizing Your Bully

Bullying is all about feelings. Most bullies are not feeling good about themselves and they try to make themselves feel better by making others feel worse. As adults we know that this strategy is doomed to fail. Positive relationships, the kind that are required to sustain long-lasting, meaningful partnerships later on in life, demand that we lift others up, not put them down. By intervening now, you will be helping your child master social skills that will serve him well throughout his life.

Where to begin? It is possible that a dislocation in your home (albeit one that is beyond your control) may have thrown your child off track. Bullies are not born, they're created. The following questions may be hard to ask, but it's important to do so:

1. *Does your son feel powerless at home?* Your son may be trying to amass power at school because he feels powerless at home. Look at the home situation from his point of view. Does he have the opportunity to feel empowered at home? Do you give him responsibilities and award him with independence when he lives up to his obligations?

2. *Is there abuse in your home?* Be honest here. If your son is being verbally or physically abused by someone in the home, he may turn around and abuse others at school.

3. *Does your son feel ignored?* If your home situation has changed (new spouse, new job, new location), you may not be able to give your son the attention he needs right now. Lacking that attention at home, he may be trying to compensate at school.

4. *Is your daughter lonely?* It takes time to make friends in middle school, particularly if she is the new kid on the block. Perhaps she returns from school to an empty home, thus increasing her sense of loneliness and isolation. Becoming a clique ringleader may be a way for her to receive the attention and adulation at school.

5. *Does your daughter have enough supervision?* While young adolescents want more independence, they also need rules. Make sure you are setting proper limits for your child. Without those boundaries at home, your child may feel there are no boundaries at school, either.

6. *Is your child struggling academically?* Middle school becomes more difficult with each passing year. Sometimes

learning problems may stand in the way of a child's success. No young adolescent wants to appear "dumb." What better way to deflect attention away from academics than to attract attention socially as the leader of a clique?

7. *Is your child worried about his physical appearance?* Young adolescents obsess about their appearance. If your daughter feels she's unattractive, she may try to be popular in other ways, by bullying others.

Talk with Your Child About Bullying

Once you discover that your child is a bully leader or follower, you want the behavior to stop *immediately*. It may not be that simple. Your bully was not created overnight. He will not be able to shed the behavior overnight, either.

Plan on having many conversations with your child over a longer period of time. It has to become your number one priority. That means sensitizing yourself to his moods and gently inquiring about events at school. Staying in touch with teachers and other parents is a must, too. It would also be a good idea to encourage him to invite friends over so that you can be the silent observer.

Your first conversation with your child will set the tone, so put some thought into what you will say. Don't be confrontational or judgmental. Try to listen more than talk. You need to have a dialogue with your daughter about her emotions. Whatever event is triggering her bullying, you must draw her out and help her find other ways to work out her issues. "Helping [children] reflect over their behavior can gently bring out their insecurities, the awkwardness that they might mask through sarcasm, bullying, and aggression," said Phillip Mountrose, in his book *Tips and Tools for Getting Through to Kids.*

If you have a specific event to talk about, start there. Here's how the conversation might flow between a father and his son, Brian:

FATHER: "I had a talk with your homeroom teacher today. She's says there's some bullying going on in the classroom. She called me because she thinks you are involved. Can you tell me about it?"

BRIAN: "It's nothing. A few of us were teasing Bobby. He's such a baby. It's just like him to run to the teacher."

FATHER: "Why were you teasing Bobby?"

BRIAN: "He's so annoying. He never sits still and he talks too much in class."

FATHER: "Well, you know Bobby has ADHD, don't you?"

BRIAN: "Yeah, I know. You can't miss that he's hyper. Why can't he control himself?"

FATHER: "He does take medication, but sometimes even with the medication he will be overly active. I think, though, that teasing him will just make the situation worse. How do you think he feels when you guys get on him?"

BRIAN: (shrugs) "Who cares?"

FATHER: "Well, maybe you should. You know that your brother, Ryan, is also ADHD. How would you feel if the kids in his class teased him?"

BRIAN: "I'd beat them up!"

FATHER: "Well, you can't always be there for Ryan. Wouldn't it be better if the kids in his class understood that Ryan had a special problem and needed their understanding rather than their criticism?"

BRIAN: "I guess."

FATHER: "I told your teacher we would have this talk and that tomorrow you would apologize to Bobby."

BRIAN: "No way!"

FATHER: "Well, if you don't apologize there will be repercussions at school and at home."

BRIAN: "That's not fair!"

FATHER: "Yes, it is. Brian, you must understand that your mother and I do not like bullying. And if you continue to act this way, then you will be punished."

BRIAN: (looks angry and upset)

FATHER: "Brian, you're a terrific kid and I love you. But I don't love your bullying behavior. It has got to stop. Understood?"

BRIAN: (nods)

This conversation must be followed up with action. Brian's dad has to stay in touch with the teachers and make sure that Brian apologizes and corrects his behavior. Brian's dad also must follow up with the other parents whose children have been following Brian's lead. He should let them know that he has had a talk with Brian and that they should talk with their sons, too. In this way, the message will get through to all the boys that what they have done is serious and will not be tolerated. Also, Brian's dad should call Bobby's parents to let them know that he does not approve of his son's behavior and has taken steps to correct it. He should ask for their help in reporting any further missteps by Brian.

Correcting Bullying Behavior

To avoid future eruptions, Brian's parents need to take stock of themselves and their children. First, Brian's parents must examine their own behavior towards Brian. Should they be spending more time with their son? Have they been showing enough interest in Brian's activities? Have they been encouraging him by praising him when he does something well? Should each parent be saying, "I love you" more often?

On a day-to-day basis, Brian's parents should implement a behavior modification program for him. How does this work? It involves calling the child on the behavior that might be considered bullying, and showing him another way to deal with his feelings. Take one example: Brian wants to borrow his brother's CD player. When Ryan says no, Brian attempts to physically bully him to get what he wants. Immediately Brian's parents should step in and point out the unacceptability of this behavior. Ryan will be hurt and angry and perhaps want to retaliate. Next time, it will be even more difficult for Brian to gain Ryan's cooperation. A better way would be to negotiate with Ryan. "If you let me use your player, I'll play ball with you later."

Brian's parents can consider other measures if Brian's negative behavior continues. One might be to seek counseling for him alone or as a family. The other might be to enroll him in a class on conflict resolution, friendship skills, or anger management. Also, a class on self-defense would be helpful. Despite what people feel, learning karate or tai kwon do doesn't teach violence but how to avoid fighting through self-control.

Lastly, Brian's parents should make sure that the school has a bully-management program in place. If not, they should lobby for one (more on lobbying for change in Step Eight).

Understand that this process is like building a house, brick by brick. But over time the result will be a solid structure that Brian can use as a foundation for forming friendships throughout his life.

No parent is excited about the prospect of raising a bully. Have faith, though, that with the right actions and words you can turn your tough guy or girl around. In the process, you will be teaching relationship skills that will last a lifetime.

Things You Can Do

Monitor your child's friendships.

Keep in touch with the school.

Network with other parents.

Tell your child you don't approve of bullying.

Things You Cannot Do

Correct bullying behavior overnight.
Use bullying behavior yourself.
Make excuses for your child's behavior.
Blame the problem on the school.

STEP FOUR

Empower Your Victim

Ten- to fifteen-year-old boys and girls live in a world where everything revolves around peers and friends. Our children unwittingly stumble onto this game board with different levels of social skill and different assets and liabilities. They learn about popularity and acceptance as they go, but most chillingly, they learn about rejection.

Nearly every young adolescent gets victimized by a peer or group of peers at some time or other during the middle school years. That is a fact of life for our children. The push and pull of social gathering during early adolescence creates outcasts and crises by the dozen. Today's friend can turn into tomorrow's tormentor. In a climate where taking pot-shots and teasing is as natural as breathing, certain children become perennial fodder for cruel sport. All of our middlers know this.

You can help your child weather her inevitable experience with rejection. In this chapter we are going to cover strategies that will empower your child when she is trapped in the victim's chair. We will show you how to:

- Use a checklist to recognize if and when your young adolescent is being vicitimized.
- Learn what type of victim role your child is trapped in so you can teach her the most effective comeback scripts.
- Look at the impression your child makes and change it, if necessary.
- Direct your young adolescent toward experiences tailored to enhance social competence and social intelligence.

You may have to give up some of the beliefs you hold about your child or what is right for your child. This isn't always going to be easy. However, as you will see, changing your ideas and giving your child new guidelines will change the way others see him, and how he is treated. Ultimately, these moves will improve how your child sees himself.

Don't Ask . . . Don't Tell

Would you know if your daughter is her clique's doormat? Do you know if your son is being tormented daily by a bully? Are you aware that your child has been struggling with rejection since kindergarten?

Many children will report when they are suffering at the hands of a vicious peer. Girls tend to come home and say, "Mom, Cindy used to be my friend. Now she is saying mean things about me. Why is she doing this to me?" Parents who are privy to these tales admit readily that they don't have all the answers.

Yet for every child who straightforwardly admits social turmoil to a parent, there are many more young adolescents who don't. Children instinctively hold back and with good reason. They don't believe confiding to a parent about being picked on will help. Furthermore, they fear that a parent will take some action that will bring more attention to their plight and make things worse. Often, they're right. Boys in particular take their social lumps and swallow their hurt. They often feel ashamed about being a victim. To admit it to mom or dad somehow compounds the shame. Since victims often blame themselves, they fear parents will heap more blame on them, too.

It can be a problem for even the most popular people. Backstreet Boy pop star Nick Carter's mom, Jane Carter, confesses as much in her best-selling book *The Heart and Soul of Nick Carter: Secrets Only a Mother Knows.* "I didn't know it then, but when Nick attended Young Junior High, his peers teased him, apparently a great deal. Bullies baited and threatened Nick, and girls—yes, even the girls—shunned him. Nick never expressed any of this to me. So you can imagine my surprise when Nick told me the truth, 'There's a side that nobody knows. I was a nerd, one of those kids who walked down the hall always with his head down. I was teased. There were fights. Honestly, if I had not had this constructive avenue to walk into with my singing, I think I might have taken a different route. It might not have been a good route.' I saw a silent apology for not telling me, his mother, any of this years ago."

Be on the lookout for any of these signs:

- Your child shows symptoms of stress such as nail-biting, bedwetting, trouble sleeping, nightmares, or stuttering. Look for emotional extremes like sadness or anger.
- Your child makes excuses—headache, stomachache, exhaustion—for not wanting to go to school. Or he starts skipping school or cutting certain classes.
- Your child slides downhill academically. She stops doing homework, hands in poor quality work, doesn't study for tests, loses motivation.
- Your child stops talking about her friends and ceases to socialize with them the way she used to. The phone has stopped ringing.
- Your child changes his routine. For example, he insists you drive him to school rather than make him take the bus. Instead of coming home after school, he goes to a friend's house. He wants you to make him lunch rather

than buy it. Didn't he complain just recently that a homemade bagged juice box and sandwich were for babies?

- Your child's life reads like a mystery. He doesn't know what happened to his science textbook, where his lunch money disappeared to, or what happened to his backpack, now muddy or ripped.
- Your child has bruises he makes light of more than once. "I bumped my cheek on my locker."
- Your child seems preoccupied with weight, height, build, or some aspect of appearance. "I want to go on a diet." "Am I ever going to start growing taller?"
- Your child asks permission to carry a knife, a can of mace, and talks about needing some form of protection. "Oh come on, Mom, you know this neighborhood isn't the safest place on earth."
- Your child talks about moving, changing schools, running away.

When you see all these clues in checklist form, it's obvious that a child is being targeted. However, in real life, many a well-meaning parent like this next one misses the signs.

"Our son is fourteen and a bright child, formerly a good student. This year first semester he *failed* one class and got a D in another. Forget the part where he should be getting nothing but A's and B's. He *isn't paying attention* or doing the work. We had him evaluated for learning disabilities or

ADD/ADHD because he is *highly disorganized.* He seems *depressed,* although the school psychologist thinks he's terrific with a wry and ironic sense of humor. He has *no close friends.* He *isn't coordinated* and we live in a very sports-oriented community. We love him so much and don't know what's behind his negative motivation or what to do."

This parent didn't add up the signs of social distress. Could being ostracized account for her boy's uncharacteristic lack of motivation? There is a likelihood that he is greeted with "Hey, egghead." In gym class, he's called "loser" and may even get his gym shorts ripped down around his knees to make the point. No wonder he can't get his academic act together.

Our point is that many of us rush around working and juggling more than one child. A ripped sweatshirt here, a failing grade for not handing in assignments there, a bad attitude; we may take notice of, and even respond to, each of these complaints without ever totalling up the evidence. There are often social explanations behind our children's problems, from lackluster school performance to disordered eating to dabbling with substance abuse.

If the checklist rings your alarm bell, set aside a quiet time to talk to your middler about being scapegoated or harassed. Try these conversation openers:

- *"Do you ever see kids getting picked on or beaten up at school?"*

  You may learn who the victims are and where children are targeted.

- *"Tell me more about the kinds of situations."*

  Florida Atlantic University expert on victimized children, Dr. David Perry, recommends tapping into children's knowledge because they are the real experts. Your child knows who gets hit, made fun of, and who is the brunt of unkind heckling.

- *"Is there a lot of name-calling?"*

  The old "Sticks and stones will break your bones, but names will never hurt you" adage is obsolete. The names tossed around today are more raw and hurtful.

- *"If something like that happened to you, would you feel comfortable telling me about it?"*

  Don't interrupt. Simply listen. Allow your child to tell you exactly what the insults are. When he is finished, recount a similar story from your own adolescent memory storehouse.

  Remember, if we don't ask our children about their experiences, they may never tell us when they are in trouble. This is where to start. If you get a sense that your child has been victimized, here's what to do next.

Born to be Riled

Before you can offer your child the help he needs, you have to figure out exactly what kind of bullying your child is faced with. Is it something about him personally, perhaps the way he looks or acts? Or is it a situation that is causing her a problem? As your child becomes more comfortable talking with you, she may volunteer more details. Chances are even then you may be required to do some detective work on your own. Observe your child's behavior. Along the way you may have to let go of some classic excuses you've made for your child. Only then will you be equipped to render the best advice and effectively empower your middler.

To help you understand your child's predicament, here are typical victim scenarios. Not all bullying looks the same. Look for your child's experiences to see which most closely resembles her troubles.

The One-Dimensional Victim: Children who are overweight or girls who develop early or become voluptuous are singled out. So are boys who are smaller than most of their classmates. Children who are head and shoulders above their peers academically get heat. Does your child possess one characteristic that makes her different? It could be a spectacular one like being particularly gifted or something seemingly insignificant to you, such as wearing glasses.

On the issues of weight, brains, and even glasses, research is divided. Studies compiled by experts insist that these features alone aren't responsible for a child being teased, but rather how a child acts in response to the taunting. Yet the real experts in these matters, the young adolescents themselves, disagree. They've reported to us that just one trait can give power mongers and bullies endless and hurtful ammunition.

The Physically Challenged Victim: Children with a physical disability or a condition like Tourette's syndrome are ripe for ridicule because their condition makes them different. Over the years parents of children who take Ritalin or other medication for learning problems have told us that their children get teased when they check in with the school nurse. Many a child has wanted to stop the medication even if it helps in order to stop the teasing. Does your child have any kind of condition that requires monitoring or medication?

Even if you think your child is handling his health issue well, he may not be. That's what this mother from Atlanta, Georgia, learned.

"I have a fifteen-year-old son who has complex partial seizures. He looks healthy and so I didn't worry too much about peers. The only time his condition becomes a problem is if he gets overexcited, overanxious, or if he overworks himself with too much exercise. Then he can have a seizure. I thought he was doing fine until he told me about gym class. He's gotten picked on a lot. The activity has either made him have a partial seizure or created anxiety. Sometimes he's had to sit out a game. Naturally, the kids riled him. Although it's not like him, he has begun to strike out verbally and even physically at his tormentors. I worry if he fights back like this he'll trigger a worse physical seizure."

A child struggling with an unusual condition inherits a double dose of stress, the condition and the ridicule. Take extra care to nourish your child's self-esteem. Empower him to change what he can and make peace with what he can't change.

The Loner Victim: Loners comes in two different kinds:

passive and aggressive. Both are likely to become chronic victims. They get teased frequently and maybe even for years.

The passive child is, in a word, shy. This child in many cases has been struggling with social stress for what seems like forever. She has trouble initiating conversations with other children. She doesn't know how to join in their games. When spoken to, she is prone to mumbling and not looking into the face of the person talking to her. Or she may not even respond at all. She doesn't feel comfortable standing up in a room, so sticking up for herself in a situation where she is being attacked is impossible. She crumbles, gives in, or withdraws.

The aggressive child is, in a word, disruptive. This child probably turns off other children with rambunctious, hyper, or aggressive behavior. He probably has a history of getting into fights or being sent to the principal's office. One of the things that can slip by unnoticed in all the drama is that this child doesn't understand other children's intentions very well. He always thinks that girls are mad at him or that boys are looking for a fight. He doesn't laugh at the right time, or he cries too often. He gets angry when the situation doesn't warrant it. Questions about him being ADD or ADHD are likely to be raised somewhere along the line.

Both types of children lack the skills to read the emotions and social cues from their peers. As a result, both can harbor obvious insecurities, short fuses, or low emotional thresholds for anxiety or tears. Bullies look for such reactions to exploit.

If you have a child with either of these temperaments, you may not have realized the implications. "Unfortunately, these are the very children whose parents are most apt to miss a cry for help," says Hara Estroff Marano, editor-at-large at *Psychology Today* and author of *"Why Doesn't Anybody Like Me?" A Guide to Raising Socially Confident Kids.* "It is extremely painful for parents to imagine that their child is disliked. So most parents of kids who wail 'I have no friends at school' are especially likely to try and dredge up evidence why it's not true rather than take the complaint seriously." So take another look and see if you have been rationalizing events that have caused your child concern.

The Accidental Victim: Many young adolescents become victims by happenstance. Their social humiliations can't be attributed to being *too* anything, too tall or too short etc. They are neither physically challenged, nor can any kind of temperamental wiring be blamed. These boys and girls are ordinary middlers who find themselves in extraordinarily unpleasant situations. This kind of victimization happens to nearly every young adolescent boy and girl at some time during the middle school years.

The situations vary. A middler is abandoned by a formerly loyal, even a best, friend. Many young adolescents come to a parting of the ways. This happens because of changing interests. One discovers the opposite sex before the other. The precocious girl moves into the dating game group. Both the girl who moves on and the one left behind suffer. The one passed over feels betrayed or devastated.

The one who moves forward can be dogged by vicious rumors.

During these years many a middler discovers and commits to developing a talent. A passion can have a price tag. Pop star Christina Aguilera told *Teen People* magazine that becoming a local celebrity after appearing in *Star Search* caused her problems. Peers threatened to beat her up and slash the tires on her mom's car. She was teased and ignored; not exactly the kind of star treatment you might expect.

Middle school also brings new people onto the scene. Realignments occur. Hard feelings tend to follow. Children this age have fragile egos and intense insecurities. Their social reflexes are clumsy and awkward. They don't have the finesse to let someone down easily and tactfully.

Going against the group is a prime way to become a target. It's commonplace for a child to be punished for not going along with the bullying or the hijinks of the moment. Does this mother who posted on our bulletin board sound familiar?

"My daughter has always been *social* and had *lots of friends.* Then her group got into drinking and smoking pot in eighth grade. My daughter said no and was crowned the outcast. She tried moving into another group; new kids, same problem. My daughter is not included now in invitations to the movies or going skating because she is no fun. The phone has stopped ringing. I know she is being put through lots of ridicule by several different girls and boys in particular. She cries to me that she just wants to be included even though she doesn't want to get high. It is so sad."

There are so many potential situations that catch our children unaware. No matter which kind of social target your child is, being in the pariah pinch is never fun.

Building a Comeback Kid

The secret to empowering each kind of victim is getting across this fact to your child: it's not who she is, or how she looks, but how she *responds* that makes or breaks the stranglehold of abuse from a clique, a ringleader, or bully. Discuss these strategies with your child so she can change the way she acts when she is targeted.

1. *Show your child that like the tango, tormenting takes two.* Dancing is a concept that young adolescents easily grasp. Explain to your child how every incident of ridicule or roughhousing requires partners just like dance partners. A tormentor and a tormentee each perform certain moves. For example, a bully demands a victim fork over his homework or lunch money; the victim surrenders the booty, quaking. Or another instance, the clique ringleader rolls her eyes, snarling, "Whatever," which translates into "You are a loser; go away." The victim smiles (dying inside) and continues talking to her, trying to impress the leader.

In the case of children who are chronic targets, the two become willing allies in the abuse. They know the routine and their respective roles by heart. You tease; I swallow it.

Why would a victimized child opt for a wimp waltz? If a child is unpopular or a loner, getting attention—even demeaning and hurtful attention from someone—proves he belongs somewhere in the social scene. Being teased is sometimes perceived as better than being ignored. The child who knuckles under a stream of "dissing" from the leader of her pack may be a black sheep, but she still is a pack member. Explain to your child that as soon as she refuses to do what is expected of her, the dance of being targeted ends.

Making a child aware of how she is responsible for her fate gives her a sense of her own power. Be sure to use the word "responsible" and explain that this is not the same thing as blame. Tell your child outright she is not to blame for being teased or shunned; the tormentor is in the wrong. However, she does play a role. Seeing her role gives her the strength and the insight to consider her other options.

2. *Write a recipe for starving the bully.* Cast the bully as "hungry" to your child. A bully feeds on a victim's responses that include crying, cowering, cringing, wincing, whining, or falling apart. When a child refuses to deliver these, then the bully gets no satisfaction. Nor does the braggart get the show that demonstrates his dominance to onlookers. Put in this way, your child realizes that he is in control, not the bully. Your child has the choice either to feed or starve his tormentor. The bully's fate is in your child's hands, not the other way around.

3. *Role-play verbal comebacks between your child and her harasser.* Practice physical reactions with your child.

- Use humor:
  BULLY: "Nice hair, NOT."
  RESPONSE: "Thanks for pointing out that I'm having a bad hair day. Did you come to school in a whirling blender, too?"

- Make the bully look stupid for not understanding the details of your medical condition:
  BULLY: "Is the school nurse on tick patrol today?"
  RESPONSE: "I take it you haven't read up on my Tourette's. You probably can't even pronounce it or spell it!"

- Confound the bully:
  BULLY: "You walk like such a pansy."
  RESPONSE: Repeat "What did you say? What does that mean?" Ask these over and over.

- Assert yourself:
  BULLY: "I'm going to tell everyone what a slut you are."
  RESPONSE: "Get out of my face or I'll report you." Shout "Go away."

4. *Alert your child to know when to run.*

In no uncertain terms, instruct your child to assess if he is going to be ambushed or hurt. If so, he should get out of the situation. We don't recommend the traditional advice given to victimized children: put up your dukes and fight back. It doesn't work. Studies affirm that bullies tend to be larger and stronger physically, and ringleaders emotionally. Victimized children are usually smaller, weaker, and less hardy emotionally and usually lose the fight, thus feeling more defeated and deflated. Another reason not to endorse fighting back is that guns and knives have been added to the bullying arsenal. Encouraging fighting teaches that violence is the best remedy. It isn't. Violence only begets more violence. Finally, sparring doesn't guarantee the end of being bullied or teased.

5. *Help your child find one supportive ally.* Children with no allies are easy prey. There really is safety in numbers. Even one friend is enough to ward off a bully. So be sure your child never travels to and from school, eats lunch, or hangs around the playground solo. If your child is being shunned by her clique, help her locate one new acquaintance. By doing so she'll envision an alternative to playing victim.

Children with a chronic illness or disability will benefit from an ally at school, but also from a support group off the premises. Finding others who share their fate imparts added strength, not to mention a store of possible comebacks that have worked for others. If you can't locate an appropriate group, the Internet has communities up and running for children with cancer, Tourette's, and many other ailments.

6. *Show your victim how others cope and triumph.* Movies are a wonderful resource to make this point. Rent classics like *Angus.* Try *Grease.* Talk about the characters. Critique the decisions the teens make in social situations. Should Sandy have undergone that juvenile delinquent makeover? Or should she have found a boy capable of appreciating her quiet and wholesome style? Did Roz handle the rumor mill

well? Other cinematic possibilities include *She's All That* and *Never Been Kissed.* Have your child read the movie reviews and make suggestions along these lines for the two of you to see together.

It's no coincidence that fifteen-year-olds are often assigned the reading of *Lord of the Flies.* Look for books, fiction or nonfiction, with themes of harassment. Try *Got Issues Much? Celebrities Share Their Traumas and Triumphs* by Randi Reisfeld and Marie Morreale. Within these pages a child learns that *Scream* sensation Neve Campbell headed up the cast as the ugliest girl in school. Neve inspired the last verse of a cruel song "Neve-aagh! Neve-aagh!" Sarah Michelle Gellar starred as the girl nobody liked. Is that where Buffy got her anti-Vampire angst? Your victim will see she is in good company.

7. *Break down social skills and practice, practice, practice.* If your child falls into that perennial victim role, he could use help to become more comfortable in social situations. Ask him: Have you felt out of sync since childhood? If the answer is yes, reassure your child that he can alter the way he behaves to make socializing easier. Work with him on recognizing facial expressions and what they mean. Go back to our feelings dictionary (Step Two). Have him describe what these feelings look like on someone's face and in their posture and how they sound. Fear raises eyebrows. Depression stoops shoulders and makes a voice sound weak. Have him demonstrate responses using his face, voice, and body language. *Teaching Your Child the Language of Social Success*

by clinical psychologists Marshall Duke and Stephen Nowicki and educator Elisabeth Martin has many examples of how to coach your child socially.

All children can build social finesse and get better at conversational repartee. A simple event like the family dinner hour can have a profound effect on social confidence. Urge your child to tell stories. This will make her more articulate. To get her to be more expressive, show her how your gestures (leaning in and looking at her) and sounds (saying, "really") demonstrate attentiveness. Conversely, practice what rude looks like. Point out the correct volume for voices. Move chairs closer to illustrate where comfort zones begin and when they are violated.

It's never too late to tackle emotional intelligence and social skill-building.

8. *Give your child the precise vocabulary to define moments of humiliation.* If another boy slammed your child into his locker and grabbed his backpack, what is that? Assault. If someone hisses "wigger" or "nigger" when your child walks by, what is that? A racial slur. If swastikas are graffiti-ed onto a child's locker, that is a bias crime. Teach your child the vocabulary that calls a crime a crime.

A fourteen-year-old Long Island girl endured such humiliation according to her mother, "The guidance counselor called me. A classmate of my daughter's sat on her, pinning her down. Then he stuck in her mouth and between her legs a penis he had fashioned from aluminum foil. On another occasion this boy stuck his hand down his pants and then rubbed something sticky all over my girl's face. My daughter told no one at first, hoping this nightmare would go away by itself."

Explain to your child that such misbehavior is not "boys will be boys"; it is sexual harassment. Review this vocabulary list that describes victimization for what it is:

sexual harassment — lewd remarks, gestures, unwanted attention, intimidation, or inappropriate touching that makes a child feel uncomfortable. Add "pantsing" (having one's pants pulled down).

assault and battery — being shoved, beaten, or stuffed in a locker. Add a "swirly" (a child is turned upside down by several others and dunked into a toilet bowl or into a trash can).

theft — being forced to hand over money or personal possessions.

bias crime — attacks or intimidation motivated by hatred of one's race, gender, or sexual orientation.

racial or ethnic slurs — insults about one's race or gender.

libel — malicious rumor.

conspiracy to commit — hearing that a group is ganging up to victimize someone.

If someone smashed you against the wall and stole your money or stuck some foreign object against you while leering, you'd do something. You'd call the authorities. Teach your child to expect and to do no less. Encourage your child to write these incidences down and report them to you, to teachers, and to administrators. When you define humiliating episodes starkly, they are less likely to be dismissed. School officials will be more likely to act, even report the behavior to law enforcement authorities.

Change the Impression Your Middler Makes

Pollsters asked twelve- to fourteen-year-olds in twenty-five cities: "What are the most important things that kids at your school use to decide who fits in?" An approximate 80% majority answered physical appearance: clothes (44%) and being good-looking (34%). Make no mistake that your child is judged by appearance. Children who look different and who ignore what's on the outside are destined to become outsiders, and oftentimes, victims.

This is a hard truth, and yet it is one that you have the power to help your child change overnight. Oh come on, you may be thinking. Can you help your child instantly? Absolutely.

Let's be honest here; we are talking about teaching your child to conform. "Conforming to style helps avoid standing out as strange or different. People in each respective group are sending the messages: 'I am a safe, predictable person to be around'; 'I am like you'; and 'You can trust me,' " according to the authors of *Teaching Your Child the Language of Social Success.* Many of us worry about conformity. We fret when we notice that our child is too eager to follow the crowd. We fear that bowing down to the group's wishes will lead our child astray, smack dab into risky behavior. We fail to take note of the fact that knowing how and when to conform is a bona fide social skill.

Your child makes a social impression. This is the image that peers hold of her based on how she looks. Your child is also graded on how she behaves; if she does what the other middlers do. Help your child blend into the norms established by her peer group. Take a mental snapshot of your child, or even a real one, and take note of the checkpoints we cover in the next few pages.

A child's look should respect the dress code. In elementary school, children are freer. A child can wear a range of pant styles, for example—from sweatpants, baggies, and corduroys to jeans—without social reprisals. In middle school, all choices narrow. Reprisals in the form of teasing widen. All of a sudden, not wearing what the others are wearing makes a child appear babyish or clueless.

What are your child's fashion choices, including items of clothing, shoes, and accessories, right down to his backpack? Compare your child's style to the fashion looks of his friends. Check out what children his age at the mall wear. Look closely at the images in magazines or clothing catalogues to see what young adolescents favor. Is your child within the norm or out of it? This does not mean we advise you to spend a fortune, or purchase clothing that you don't approve of, such as midriff-bearing tops. Just make a change here and there, adjustments that you can both live with. You'd be surprised how one new pair of baggy jeans or a fresh pair of sneakers can update his appearance, and upgrade how others see him.

Pay attention to undergarments at this age, too. Girls develop at different ages and are very sensitive whether they are early or late bloomers. Help your daughter fit in if it means buying her a training bra before she needs it. Make sure she isn't a target because of bouncing breasts. A very young girl whose breasts are growing more quickly than her peers is bound to be self-conscious. In one survey, by age seven, 7% of white girls and 27% of girls of color had begun to show signs of puberty. Your daughter may need your gentle guidance in the decision-making department and in the bra-shopping department, too.

There are plenty of other things to consider, too. Is your son's hairstyle planned? Does your daughter spend time thinking about which barrettes are hot? Some do and some don't. Yet the child who takes no care grooming his or her hair may get teased. We say *grooming* rather than *combing* for a reason. The cuts these days often involve sticky spikes, sections of the head braided or shaved, a deliberate just-woke-up messy look, or locks dangled across the forehead. Make an appointment and get your child a new haircut if necessary. That may mean getting only an inch trimmed off and a reshaping. Getting a fresh cut or a few highlights isn't drastic, but can be very flattering. Others will notice.

Don't ignore the issue of facial or body hair either. Some boys have dark mustache growth as early as fifth or sixth grade. While a mother is thinking: *He's too young to shave*, peers are dubbing him "*Chewbacca*" (the hairy creature from *Star Wars.)* There is no right age for your boy to start shaving. Or for that matter, your girl, if she shows dark hair above her lips. When a girl announces she wants to shave her legs, it's because she noticed others doing so or because others have teased her. Pay attention to when and where your child is developing hair, how it looks, and whether you need to allow them to do something about it.

Many mothers and daughters get into warfare over when it's time to wear lipstick, use eyeliner, or eye shadow. Listen to your daughter's desires. Don't automatically insist, "You are too young to wear that face paint!" Look at what her friends are wearing. Compromise. A ten-year-old may indeed be too young for a Cindy Crawford full-face palette of darkened brows and rouge, but she may be old enough for lip gloss or some face sparkle. If you don't think her look is appropriate for school, say so, but allow her to doll up a little for special occasions or weekends. Young girls long to be older. Wearing makeup satisfies this yearning. So does smoking cigarettes. Think about which is safer to endorse.

If your daughter is applying makeup incorrectly or too liberally, take her to a department store at the mall for a cosmetic demonstration. Or invite a Mary Kay consultant in for a lesson. Get a video. Let her practice. You want her to take pride in her appearance. Her peers do.

Jewelry items change with the trends—one earring or two. What are your son's friends wearing? An earring is a hot button for many parents, especially those with bejeweled boys. Children experiment with different looks at this age. An earring is an adventure, a walk on the wild side. It's a better expression of rebellion than smoking a joint. Keep that in mind.

This is not to say you have to endorse "the everybody's doing it" body piercing rage which includes everything from nose rings to bellybutton diamonds. Use your common sense. Help your child develop some of that, too. Find a bracelet, necklace, or wristwatch that can make her trendy, similar to the tastes of her friends.

Unwashed is never cool. For many of today's adolescents, pajamas are passé. They fall into bed in street sweats, or shorts and T-shirts. You may not want to admit it to anyone but yourself, but your middler has been known to tumble into bed, out of bed the next morning, and off to school in the same clothes, socks included. Bad timing on the socks especially. Middlers hold the *Guinness*-like distinction for having the smelliest feet of a lifetime, boys more so than girls. Let your child pass on traditional pj's, but make sure he starts the day in clean clothes.

Take a close look at your child's hair every day for a week. Is she in the habit of keeping it clean? Does she wash her face? Is she bathing regularly? Is teeth brushing and dental flossing a part of the morning routine? Does she put on deodorant daily without fail? "*Children who have hygiene problems are usually unaware of the expressive power of their poor personal hygiene* [authors' italics]; they are simply oblivious to the reasons behind any avoidance or teasing," say Duke, Nowicki, and Martin in their *Teaching Your Child the Language of Social Success.*

Another reason for hygiene lapses is their age and one of

its hazards, fatigue. Their body clocks are resetting to a later mode and they go to sleep later. School begins earlier and our children have to rise earlier. This adds up to many of them being tired morning, noon, and night. Middlers have homework, too, and TV shows to watch. Boys and girls have gossip to share on the telephone or on the Internet. All young adolescents tend to be disorganized and forgetful. Good hygiene can and does get lost in the shuffle. "I'm too tired to take a bath tonight." "I don't have time to shower this morning—I'll be late." Suggest your child find a new bath or shower routine if need be. But be careful not to turn hygiene into a control issue.

Oily skin is part of early adolescence, as hormones fluctuate. Bad complexions happen. If your child is suffering from a flare-up of pimples, take her to the dermatologist. There are many new prescription products not sold over the counter that can effectively clear up troubled skin. These can erase facial scars, and with them, the emotional scars of being teased.

Good hygiene makes a good impression. An added bonus is that it teaches our children to take good care of their bodies. This nurturing of the physical self reverses some of the body loathing and self-consciousness that plague children at this age. So give them tissues for their backpack, an extra sanitary napkin, and a breath-freshening aid like Altoids, Tic Tacs, or other breath mints. Habits also have a way of establishing order at a time when our young so often feel out of control.

Give Your Child a Foothold on Common Ground

All of our children are card-carrying members of their own youth subculture. Certain TV shows, CDs, video games, magazines, and other media experiences are the touch points. Is everyone in your child's circle playing the latest video game? TV stars and story lines set the buzz among young adolescents. There are everyday rituals. Going home to instant message one another on the computer after school is as familiar to the net generation as turning on the TV set was in the '60s and '70s.

Just as you need to give your child permission to look the part, you need to allow him to act the part. Many parents enforce boundaries that may be too restrictive. For example, you may disapprove of violent video games and prohibit your son from buying any of them. You may think telephone calls coming in all night are unnecessary, not to mention spending hours on AOL (sometimes with the phone crooked in her neck while her fingers are doing the electronic walking simultaneously). You may have caught a rap song on MTV, found yourself appalled, and decided to ban rap music.

If your middler is prevented from having access to the media entertainment and rituals that his peers experience, he will wind up out of the loop. He then lacks the common ground of cultural points of reference. We are *not* saying that every rap artist, TV drama, video game, or middler communication timetable is correct. However, we are advising that parents be flexible on some video games or popular entertainers, or else your child won't know what the other young adolescents are crazy over or giggling about. He will be exiled or labeled as "out of it." On the other hand, if he knows the shows, games, and routines, he becomes just like his peers and shares their subculture.

The push and pull over TV, websites, R-rated movies, or going to live music concerts is just beginning. Start with an attitude that enables you to stand behind your values, yet allows your child some leeway to explore. Your role is to help him process and choose media. The operative word is "compromise."

The Courage to Be More Social

A child must display courage to triumph over bullying. Your child needs courage, but not the physical kind. He needs social courage. The way to develop this kind of bravado is by building up your child's social competence and confidence. Try providing these opportunities:

Organize a family reunion with your middler. Children of yesterday had a large web of family connections at their fingertips. A nearby extended family of grandparents, aunts, uncles, and cousins translated into many afternoons of socializing with relatives of all ages and temperaments. Nowadays families are scattered, and children have fewer family gatherings in which to develop automatic social competence. And those relatives that they do spend time with, unlike classmates, have only goodwill toward the child.

None of us can go back to the days of close-knit extended families, but we can corral a spread-out family to bring back that safe, social training ground. Put your young adolescent in charge of the guest list. Let him e-mail invitations or send them by snail mail. Encourage him to tally the RSVPs. This will surely entail conversational catching up with relatives from near and far. Have him suggest games, a family reunion photograph shoot, even a newsletter to update everyone. The anticipation and planning will distract him from social jitters before the event. The event itself will offer a day of social experiences and links that may continue long after.

If your family is small, contemplate other kinds of reunions. What ever happened to your daughter's first play group or ballet troupe, or your son's first little league or scout troop? The idea is to create a bash with peers and adults who are out of the usual social loop.

Look for episodes of spontaneous unsupervised play. As children, we hopped on bicycles and rode to the playground for informal games. Or we simply stepped outside onto the street for impromptu rounds of hopscotch, kickball, or hide-and-seek. Just going "out to play" like we did is extinct in countless communities.

The play of today's children is planned by parents and supervised by adults from preschool through high school. Sports like softball or soccer kick off seasonally among town team players coached by adults and supervised by referees. Children graduate from play dates to sleep over parties, but both share adult supervision and a lack of spon-

taneity. That old rough-and-tumble of neighborhood kids interacting built a sense of social roles, experience, and comfort.

Be on the lookout for this kind of adult-free play. Nudge your middler toward any such spontaneous games in the neighborhood or when you are at parties. These opportunities teach them how to become part of an instant team. These may be the loosey-goosey teams, but fitting in adeptly builds lasting good feelings and confidence.

Enroll your child in one of the martial arts. After a talk, the parent of a child who fails at sports and who is teased unmercifully asked us, "Why don't they have assertiveness training for children?" While few communities offer such workshops formally for the ten- to fifteen-year-old set, assertive behavior is part of martial arts classes. From karate to tae kwan do, popular among both boys and girls, these classes deliver several social advantages. They firm up the body, giving a child a better body image. They don't teach fighting, but do teach assertive body language and self-defense. They underscore both emotional and physical control and enhance self-esteem by making a child feel stronger and safer.

When all is said and done, our victimized sons and daughters benefit from our vigilance and can be empowered under our guidance. Above all, they are strengthened by our reassurance.

Things You Can Do

Assess whether your child is a likely target or an occasional victim.

Identify character traits and behaviors that set him apart.

Practice techniques to stump bullies and ringleaders.

Work with your child to improve social skills and communication ability.

Multiply his opportunities to practice socializing.

Things You Cannot Do

Protect your child from ever being victimized.

Change his personality or temperament.

Force the middlers in his class to view him fairly and treat him kindly.

Arrange friendships for your child.

STEP FIVE

Get Your Bystander to Participate

The best way to eliminate cliques and bullies is to encourage the silent majority to speak up. Those kids who stand on the sidelines, watching other children be humiliated, hold the key to reform in their hands. As the saying goes, "If you're not part of the solution, you're part of the problem." Standing by silently reaffirms the clique's power. Speaking up nullifies it.

Yet it isn't easy for any child to muster the necessary courage and get involved. He fears being hurt or targeted next. He worries that he will lose friends. He also wonders whether the adults will believe his version of the story. For all these reasons, we have to teach our children the correct way to intervene.

In this chapter, we will:

- Make you aware of the important role the bystander plays in clique-land.
- Outline how the media encourage children to watch rather than act.
- Give you ways to talk with your child about getting involved.
- Help you turn your child into a catalyst for change.

One study done about children and bullying in Canada found that 43% of the students said that they try to help the victim; 33% said they should help but don't, and 24% said that bullying was none of their business. In other words, less than half of the children got involved, while 57% did nothing. With those kinds of statistics, cliques will thrive.

The Role of the Bystander

Where cliques are concerned, an innocent bystander is an oxymoron. As long as a person stands by and allows others to be harmed, he is not innocent. Some states and cities, in fact, have passed legislation making it illegal to watch a crime happen and not act. Here's why it's even more important for children to get involved:

Bystanders have a numerical advantage. "Though there is conflicting data about the percentage of children who are identified as victims, the majority of students in a given classroom are neither bullies nor victims, they are witnesses to the bullying," according to Suellen Fried and Paula Fried, in their book *Bullies and Victims: Helping Your Child Through the Schoolyard Battlefield*. The corollary of this is that there is strength in numbers. If the bystanders get involved, they can make a difference.

Bystanders can turn a situation around. They can stop what is happening by calling attention to the action or by seeking the help of an adult. Because the bystanders are not the actual targets, their opinions can be viewed as more objective and therefore, more powerful.

Bystanders can suffer psychologically. "Children who are spectators in the arena of bullying will not be unscathed," said Fried and Fried. "The conflict they experience can lead to feelings of sadness, anger, guilt, and shame." Just because our children are not the ones being tortured, it doesn't mean they are not being harmed. The knowledge that "I should have done something" is enough to create psychological distress.

Bystanders are rarely neutral. Even though they stand on the sidelines, when they fail to intervene they are condoning the activities of the clique. Remaining idle isn't something that kids can do for a long time. Therefore, most bystanders eventually become more active participants, backing up the clique leaders to various degrees.

As parents, we can't be bystanders, either. We can't stand by watching our children fight these battles alone. We must arm them with the right words and the right actions, and we must be there when they need back-up.

When Bystanders Turn Violent

Perhaps the most compelling argument for parents to get involved was spelled out in a Justice Department report released in 2000 which found that juveniles are twice as likely as adults to commit serious crimes in groups. In April 2000, the *New York Times* conducted its own study which concurred with the government's findings. The *Times* found that while adult "rampage" killers were "loners" who planned their crimes secretively, school-age killers actively sought out peer support for their plans and often bragged about their intentions beforehand.

Numerous cases illustrate these findings in tragic detail. In April 1996, four teens from Fort Myers, Florida, went on a crime spree that included arson and robbery, and culminated in the brutal murder of a popular high school teacher. One of the killers, an eighteen-year-old honor student, had been given a $20,000 college scholarship and aspired to work at NASA. "The boys individually would never do anything like this," said Detective Lt. Gil Allen of the Lee County Sheriff's Department. "But the group gave them an identity."

Other youthful killers have acted in tandem. Andrew Golden, eleven, and Mitchell Johnson, thirteen, carried out the shootings in Jonesboro, Arkansas, which left four children and a teacher dead, and ten others wounded. And, in Littleton, Colorado, Eric Harris, eighteen, and Dylan Klebold, seventeen, went on a killing spree and killed twelve students, a teacher, and then themselves.

Even if youthful killers don't entice others to join in, they appear eager to have their peers witness their handiwork. In 1997, Evan Ramsey, sixteen, shot a popular basketball player in the stomach. Classmates at his high school in Bethel, Alaska, watched from the balcony above, having been alerted by Ramsey the day before that he would stage "an evil act." No one alerted authorities.

Suffering on the Playing Fields

Peer pressure also plays a role in the escalating violence of hazing which usually involves school athletes. There has been a rash of such incidents:

- In March 2000, fourteen players on a Baltimore high school soccer team dragged freshmen across a muddy field and forced them to stand against a wall while being whacked by soccer balls kicked at close range. Two students were injured, one suffered a concussion.
- In fall, 1999, on Long Island, New York, the season opener for the Great Neck South High School football team was forfeited after ten players were suspended for beating a freshman player, leaving him severely bruised.

- In 1999, at a football camp on Staten Island, New York, high school students from New Jersey and Long Island were roughed up, paddled on their rear ends, and forced to box each other until they bled.
- In early 1999, a high school wrestling team in Trumbull, Connecticut, with a decades-long tradition of hazing, drew the attention of police after a fifteen-year-old boy's bruises were noticed by his parents.

Hazing is no longer viewed as an adolescent prank, but as vicious, violent, and sometimes deadly. Dr. Rachel Lauer, a psychologist at Pace University who has studied hazing, said that kids participate because they are eager to belong to a group. "In addition to companionship and comfort, there's a certain amount of prestige in belonging," she said. "And the harder it is to get in, the more prestigious it is."

Parents need to know that children who remain passive risk being sucked into the activity in a negative way. Those who take a stand are in a better position to resist.

What the Bystander Looks Like

The typical profile of the bystander is someone who, literally, stands by while the action happens. In reality, bystanders assume different roles in clique-land. Some of these roles are closer to the action than others. Occasionally, bystanders get in on the action, too, but they never assume the starring roles. Think of them as the supporting actresses and actors in our schoolhouse drama. Do you recognize your child in any of the following character sketches?

Gwyneth Pal-to-All. This bystander tries to stay neutral by being a friend to everyone. It's a demanding role, particularly when the clique leader targets certain kids. Rather than stand up to the bullies, this gal-pal will play both sides of the fence, sympathizing with the victims and the leaders. She gives false hope to the victims and tacit approval to the bullies.

Greta Garble. Gossiping is the favorite pastime for this bystander. She may never start a hurtful rumor, but has no reservation about passing it along, usually in an altered form.

George Clue-Less. If he stopped to think about what he was doing, this bystander would understand how his actions harm others. But he has more important issues on his mind (which CD to buy, who to ask to the movies, what chat room he should visit) than to actually analyze his behavior.

Jennifer Angst. This bystander becomes noticeably distressed whenever she is exposed to clique activities. She hates seeing her classmates tortured. Often after a rough day watching the social machinations at her school, she arrives home feeling sad, guilty, angry, and tired.

Jack Nichols-and-Dimes. This guy's loyalty can be bought for a price. On numerous occasions he has remained silent or backed up the clique leader in front of adults. He puts up; the bully pays up. The opportunities are endless and his resourcefulness has helped him build up an impressive CD collection.

Meg Ryle-Em. Stirring the pot is what this bystander does best. If the clique leader is about to let up on a victim, she will innocently remind the bully of a recent incident sure to churn up old anger. Later, she will even reassure the victim that she did everything to stop the bully.

Many bystanders really don't understand the hurtful nature of their actions. They don't view themselves as leaders or followers, bullies or victims. If pressed, they would agree that they belong to one group or another, yet they would eschew any involvement in the nasty goings-on that characterize cliques.

Surviving in Clique-Land

Once a parent sees his child in one of these bystander roles, he might be quick to dole out criticism or punishment. Before you do that, however, take some time to understand what motivates your child. Bystanders are not born; they are made. Your child, like others in the class, is adapting to his environment.

We like to think that our children go to school to get a good education and prepare for college. That's true, but much more goes on inside those brick walls from 8 A.M. to 3 P.M. The social drama is riveting and distracting. Even the best students can get sidetracked when they are subjected to ridicule and scorn.

If the truth be told, many of us could probably remember our own struggles to fit in. It's important that we awaken those feelings in ourselves so that we can empathize with the plight of our children.

One mother tells this tale about what happened to her in tenth grade:

"Jane, the leader of a group of popular kids, liked a boy named Greg. They had been together for several months when he asked another girl, Penny, to the movies. Penny and I had been friends for a long time and, while we were not members of the popular group, we were definitely on the fringes. Of course, when Greg asked Penny to the movies and she accepted, she was targeted by Jane and all of Jane's group.

"We were at the local hangout, a soda fountain, and I chose to sit in a booth with Jane rather than in another booth with Penny. Jane and her friends started saying horrible things about Penny so that everyone in the place could hear. And I joined in. Why? I'm ashamed to admit it, but I was afraid to stand up for Penny. My position in the group wasn't that secure and I know I would have been targeted next. It was self-preservation, pure and simple. But even today, I think about that incident and feel tremendous guilt."

Most of us could delve into our adolescent pasts and come up with similar anecdotes. In fact, many of us have probably run into similar situations in our work life, times when we were afraid to back up a co-worker even when we knew he was right because we feared being penalized by the boss.

As the mother in the example above discovered, self-preservation often involves compromising your values to avoid being singled out for abuse. One-on-one, this mother never would have insulted her friend. Once she sat down with Jane rather than Penny, however, she essentially chose sides. Of course, she could have remained silent, but even so, her physical presence showed that she sympathized with Jane rather than Penny. Why did she join in verbally abusing Penny? No doubt she became caught up in the group's frenzy. Perhaps she was pressured by the group into saying something. Whatever her reasons, her actions haunt her to this day.

The Negative Influence of the Media

In previous chapters we have talked about how movies and TV shows validate clique-like behavior, essentially turning clique leaders and bullies into role models and heroes. The media have another effect, however, one that directly influences children to become bystanders. Listen to the following report from a father:

"My son went to an eighth-grade dance which drew children from many different schools. One kid and several of his friends went around threatening some of the boys, including my son. One of my son's friends came to his rescue. His reward? This bully and his posse jumped the boy in the coat room and beat him up. When my son returned home and told me what had happened, his comment alarmed me. He said, 'Dad, watching Brian get beaten up was like watching a video game.' He wasn't the only kid who just watched. I was sickened that these kids, my son included, didn't jump in to help their friend. They were mesmerized by watching real violence and felt it wasn't real."

Children who watch violent programming become immune to it. "When violent acts on television are repetitive or exceedingly graphic, some young viewers may become desensitized and callous to other forms of real suffering," said Dr. Helen Boehm, who has studied children's viewing patterns for more than twenty years and has served as an advisor to various media producers. In her book, *Viewing Violence,* Madeline Levine notes that in order for a person to react quickly in an emergency situation, he must first remain sensitive to the dangers. A child whose media diet consists of large doses of violence will be less likely to be frightened by the real thing. That means he will choose to watch rather than act when he sees someone who needs help.

In fact, some kids not only don't help, they also videotape the action themselves. In October 1999, sixty students from an upstate New York high school faced criminal prosecution after they cheered on two other students who settled a grudge in a fight that was videotaped by one of the students. The two fighters, both fifteen, were taken in and faced possible assault charges. The six-minute video allowed the police to identify the students who formed a human boxing ring around the two fighters. Police felt that the fight had been planned at least a day in advance and that no one had tried to get adults involved to stop it. The crowd ranged in age from fourteen to twenty-one and included twenty girls.

Most parents worry that watching brutal TV shows and movies will make a child more violent. Yet few of us worry about the opposite effect, that constantly being exposed to violent acts will anesthetize our children, making it difficult, if not impossible, for them to intervene in a positive way. How do we prevent that from happening? We need to intervene to counter the negative messages they receive from the media. Here are some ideas:

1. *Stress the difference between watching and doing.* Life is not a spectator sport. Whenever you have the opportunity, promote doing over watching. Rather than watch a home repair show on TV, start a project in your home and get your young adolescents involved.

2. *Draw a line between fiction and reality.* TV dramas are punched up to create more excitement. This is entertainment and doesn't demand our involvement. Watch with your child and make that point.

3. *Talk about the choices made by characters on TV.* Role-play with your child when watching TV. "What would you do if you saw someone being bullied by kids in your class?" Your child can't control the actors on the screen, but he can make a difference in his own world. Make sure he understands the difference.

Finding Out Where Your Child Stands

You probably know your child's friends, those he spends most of his time with in and out of school. What you might not know is whether he and those friends are bystanders in clique-land. Of course, you could come right out and ask your child, but chances are he won't understand what his role is, and even if he does, he won't be quick to tell you.

In order to learn more, you have to talk with him about his friends and friendships. As a first step, network with other parents and talk with your son's teachers to get an idea of what is going on in the classrooms and corridors at school. This information will help you shape your dialogue.

Let's say that you hear there has been a fight at school among some of the boys. Your son wasn't one of the fighters, so why should you be concerned? First, because you don't know if he won't be involved next time. Second, you know that schoolyard fights sometimes involve weapons and can easily result in serious injury or death, even to bystanders. Third, you know that bystanders can suffer trauma from watching a fight. Fourth, as a responsible parent you want your son to understand that he can influence the actions of others in a positive way.

You need to find out what role your son played. Here's an example of how the conversation might go:

DAD: "I was talking to Jeremy's dad today and he said that there was a fight at school last week. Were you there?"

OLIVER: (shrugs) "I might have been."

DAD: "Well, either you were there or you weren't, Oliver. Were you there?"

OLIVER: (sighs) "Yeah, I was there."

DAD: "Who was fighting?"

OLIVER: "Nick and Matt."

DAD: "Do you know why they were fighting?"

OLIVER: (shrugs again) "Over something stupid."

DAD: "Well, obviously it was serious to the boys or they wouldn't have fought."

OLIVER: "Yeah, well, Nick told everyone that Matt's father lost his job. He called Mr. Dawson a loser."

DAD: "That must have made Matt angry."

OLIVER: "It made a lot of us angry. Mr. Dawson's not a loser. He coached our baseball team last year and helped us win first place."

DAD: "So who started the fight?"

OLIVER: "Matt tried to get Nick to take back what he said. But he just said meaner things. So Matt told Nick to meet him in the parking lot after school."

DAD: "What did you think was going to happen?"

OLIVER: "I thought they would fight. Everyone did."

DAD: "Did you try to talk Matt out of fighting?"

OLIVER: (shakes his head) "I knew he wouldn't listen to me. He just wanted to get back at Nick."

DAD: "How about alerting one of the teachers?"

OLIVER: "I didn't want to get Matt in trouble. He's the one who asked for the fight. And Nick would make sure the teachers knew that."

DAD: "Did you watch the fight?"

OLIVER: (nods) "It was bad. Matt's so much smaller than Nick. He was all bloody."

DAD: "His dad told me he had four stitches on his forehead."

OLIVER: "I should have said something. It's my fault he got hurt. He's my friend. I should have done something."

DAD: "Well, fortunately Matt wasn't injured seriously. But, Oliver, let's think about this, because you know, it may happen again, perhaps not with Matt and Nick, but with someone else."

OLIVER: "You think I should have told someone?"

DAD: "Is there a teacher at school you trust?"

OLIVER: (nods) "Yeah, Mr. Brennan. He would have gotten Nick to apologize and they wouldn't have had the fight."

DAD: "Oliver, it's not your fault they fought. But sometimes when kids get angry they don't think clearly. That's why it's important for kids who aren't directly involved, like you, to do the thinking for them. Do you understand?"

OLIVER: "I think so. I should have gotten more involved to help Matt. I will next time."

Sometimes the incident may not be a fight, but more subtle intimidation doled out over time. If kids stand by, those who are being singled out may suffer. Here's the conversation a parent may have to talk about such a situation:

MOTHER: "I saw your science teacher, Mrs. Knoll, when I was at the school yesterday. She told me that Annette Coles is being teased by some girls at school. Did you know that?"

STACEY: "Yeah, it's mostly Candy and Kristen. They make fun of her clothes."

MOTHER: "Well, I know the Coles don't have much money. Annette probably can't afford the latest stuff."

STACEY: "Mom, she only has one pair of pants. That's why they make fun of her. They say she doesn't wash her clothes because she seems to wear almost the same thing every day."

MOTHER: "What does Annette do when they make fun of her?"

STACEY: "She tries to ignore them, but that's hard when they keep at her."

MOTHER: "How do you think Annette feels when Candy makes fun of her?"

STACEY: "Awful. I would. And it's not even her fault she can't afford better clothes."

MOTHER: "You know, there's an old saying, 'The clothes don't make the man.' What's important is the person inside."

STACEY: "I know, Mom. And Annette really is very nice."

MOTHER: "Don't any of the girls stick up for her?"

STACEY: "Everyone's too scared."

MOTHER: "Of Candy?"

STACEY: "Mom! You don't know how mean she can be. Once Mary Beth refused to share her English homework and Candy told everyone that Mary Beth had lice. By the end of the day, even the teacher believed it and made Mary Beth go to the nurse's office to be checked out."

MOTHER: "Well, I realize it may be tough to stand up to Candy alone. What if you and some of your friends did it together?"

STACEY: "Like if Nancy and Jenny joined with me?"

MOTHER: "Right."

STACEY: "I don't know, Mom."

MOTHER: "Well, I know that Mrs. Knoll would also back you up."

STACEY: (thinking) "I could try to say something in science class. That's usually where Candy embarrasses Annette."

MOTHER: "Perhaps if the three of you disagree with Candy, others in the class will, too."

STACEY: "They might. No one likes what she's doing to Annette. Okay, Mom. I'll try it."

While the parents in these two examples are dealing with one incident, when you encourage your child to get involved you are establishing a pattern you hope she will follow in the future. The next time your son hears about a fight, or whenever your daughter watches someone being taunted, stepping in will become their automatic response.

Helping Your Bystander Intervene

When children step in, they can effect change. Listen to this mother who posted this on our message boards:

"Someone in my daughter's class was saying nasty things about her. Unfortunately, she said these things in front of some people who like my daughter. They reported this girl. All were asked to write down what was done and said. The assistant principal asked the harasser to write down her version. There was enough material to punish her. She received two detention reports which require two Saturday school visits."

There are many methods a child can use to discourage the meanness that occurs in our schools. Brainstorm with your child. You may discover he has already given the subject some thought and will surprise you with his approach.

1. *Don't watch.* The clique leader wants an audience. Don't give her one. Walk away.

2. *Don't react.* If it's not possible to leave (say your child is in class or on the bus), refusing to laugh or endorse the clique leader's action with words may shut him down.

3. *Don't gossip.* Passing on rumors—in notes, whispers, or e-mails—can hurt feelings and may even escalate the conflict to violence.

4. *Combat gossip with the truth.* Gossip can take on a life of its own and damage a child's reputation. Calling a girl a "slut," for example, will not only hurt her feelings, but may make her a target for boys who really believe she is

"easy." Challenging the gossip-monger will stop the rumor mill.

5. *Offer verbal support in private.* Your child may not feel courageous enough to confront a bully in public, but he can still talk with the victim later on and let him know he cares. "I heard what Jessie said about being adopted. I just wanted you to know that I have a cousin who was adopted and she is terrific. So don't take Jessie's comment seriously. She doesn't know what she's talking about."

6. *Offer other support.* Sometimes a child being picked on could benefit from some help. "I heard Mark making fun of you because you flunked the math test. Math's my best subject. I could help you, if you like."

7. *Offer support in front of the clique leader.* Sometimes this can involve merely standing beside the child being targeted. Other times saying something will be necessary. For example, if the clique leader makes fun of the victim's clothes, the bystander could say: "You know, I have a skirt like that, but I haven't worn it for a while. I'll dig it out and wear it soon."

8. *Gather others.* A clique leader will have a more difficult time tormenting someone if several kids in the class leap to the child's defense. This back-up response could be spontaneous or planned. "Hedy is always picking on Rebecca at lunch. What do you say we all eat with her today so Hedy will stay away?"

9. *Align with the victim.* If a child is being picked on for a specific reason (for being a slow runner, for example), the bystander can put himself into the same category. "I'm a

slow runner, too, Sam. Maybe we could run together sometime to see if we can get better."

10. *Work with the victim.* Kids are targeted for different reasons. Sometimes a child is the last one to know what irritating habit causes him to be singled out. A bystander can gently point out this fact. "I know you get upset when Terry makes fun of you in class, but the way you always call out the answers before anyone else annoys a lot of the kids. Do you think you could wait until the teacher calls on you?"

11. *Create a distraction.* Sometimes the bully picks on someone in order to draw attention to himself. But if he has to compete with a bystander who has created a diversion, he might lose his focus and stop his teasing. For example, if a group is in a lunchroom and the bully is making fun of the victim's brown bag lunch, the bystander can tell a joke.

12. *Use humor.* Making light of a situation when things heat up is a good way to diffuse the tension. The best strategy is for your child to make himself the object of the humor. "Boy, you don't like the way Jerry is dressed today. Wait until you see me tomorrow in my grandfather's overalls."

13. *Extend an invitation.* Sometimes a child who is being teased will become discouraged and isolate herself from others. Reaching out may help her connect again. "Some of us are going to the movies this weekend. Would you like to come?"

14. *Start an on-line support group.* Young adolescents are spending more of their time in cyberspace. This venue provides a perfect arena to lend support to anyone who has

been targeted. Your daughter could invite someone who has been victimized to join in a chat or instant messaging session. Once kids talk together on-line, their friendships often spill over to the classroom.

15. *Appeal to the clique leader.* If done in the right way by the right child, this approach can work. "I heard you saying mean things to the new girl, Molly. She lives near me so I've gotten to know her. I think if you knew her better, you'd like her, too. I'm having her over Friday night for pizza and a movie. Do you want to come?"

16. *Keep a record.* Memories fade fast, especially for kids. If your child tells you about someone in the class who is operating a clique, encourage him to write down incidents and include the place, time, and people involved.

17. *Confront the bully.* Sometimes a more aggressive approach is needed. But advise your child to do so cautiously because the bully may try to retaliate. Tell your child not to approach the bully alone and to make sure a teacher is nearby in case he needs to call for help. Your son could tell the bully, "What you said to John during gym class was mean and unfair. It made a lot of us mad." (The other boys accompanying your son, can show they agree.) "You should think before you say something like that again."

18. *Get a teacher involved.* If the action occurring is violent, your child should opt for grabbing the nearest teacher. Oftentimes the child will want a teacher to know when a child is being taunted because it not only is hurting the victim but also affecting other children as well. In this case,

your child should think carefully about which teacher could be counted on to handle the situation properly.

19. *Get a parent involved.* There may be some situations that can only be solved with parents getting involved. Why would you want to do so when the child being targeted is not your own? Well, if your child comes to you for help, it means she is distressed enough to be adversely affected by the clique goings-on. You should, however, think carefully about your approach. That's what we'll deal with now.

How to Intervene as a Parent

If your own child was being targeted by a clique, your reason to get involved would be clear and your approach straightforward. It's a bit more tricky when your child is a bystander. Some people might question your motives. Some may not take you seriously. But if you feel you should get involved, here are some ideas to help you devise a game plan:

1. *Make sure you have all the facts.* You have heard the story from your child, but she may not have all the information you need to make a judgment. So spend some time as a clique detective. Attend the next PTA meeting and listen to other parents. Gently inquire about problems in the class.

2. *Talk with other parents.* Follow up by having one-on-one talks with any parents who are closer to the action. You might want to take an indirect approach so you don't seem to be confrontational. "I hear there are some social

issues developing in our daughters' class. What have you heard?"

3. *Go to the source: the kids themselves.* Help your daughter arrange a get-together with some of her friends. The gathering may or may not include some of the clique members and victims. If the major players are present, you will be able to observe their interactions for yourself. If they are not there, you will still have the opportunity to eavesdrop on conversations while you pass around the soda and chips.

4. *Decide whom you will approach.* Should you go to the school? Would a conversation with a parent help? This is a judgment call. If you know any of the parents well, then talking with them might be the way to go. Be sure that you consider carefully how you will frame the discussion. Don't assign blame or be critical. Making statements like, "If you gave Anne more attention at home, maybe she wouldn't be so mean to other kids," will only be greeted with hostility and non-cooperation. Instead, express your concern that all the children need to learn how to get along. How can you, as parents, accomplish that?

5. *Take your case to the school.* If talking with parents isn't possible or fails, then you may have no choice but to go to the school. Usually the assistant principal is in charge of discipline, but going directly to that person may be overlooking others who know more about the situation. Is there one teacher (homeroom or gym, for example) you know who has witnessed some of the incidents? You might want to start there.

6. *Be honest about why you are intervening.* Your child has

told you some of what has been happening. She is upset and you want to see if there is anything you, and other parents, can do to turn the situation around. If the teacher is ignorant of what has been happening, fill her in without implicating specific children. It's her job to investigate once you have told her there is a problem.

7. *Once you have informed the school, disengage.* Hopefully your heads-up will alert the powers-that-be. After a week, check in with your child. Does she think the situation has improved? If after two weeks, things have not gotten any better, you may have to make a follow-up call to school, perhaps seeking out someone with greater authority.

Working Long-term on Your Bystander

We said earlier in this chapter that bystanders are made, not born. Social pressures at school inhibit some children from getting involved. There is much we can do over time, however, to teach our children to become social activists where friendships are concerned. Here are some ideas:

1. *Turn off the TV.* When children gather at your house, discourage TV watching. "Children need to learn how to have fun, talk, and solve problems with other children," said Fred Frankel in his book, *Good Friends Are Hard to Find*. "Watching TV together with others or playing videogames for most of the play date prevents this, since the children learn little about each other."

2. *Turn on the TV.* There are many shows aimed at teenagers. Watch one with your child and have her record

how many times characters "dis" each other. Does that happen at her school? You will help her understand the hurtful nature of cliques.

3. *Downplay popularity and good looks.* Too much emphasis on these attributes skews how children view their classmates. Instead, ask your daughter what sports her friends like, what books they read, what they do to help others.

4. *Consider feelings.* Children who are able to recognize their own feelings are also able to relate to friends in distress.

After a talk we gave in Maryland, one mother approached us about an experience she had that influenced her son. She was asked to testify for a co-worker in a discrimination case in her office. Even before the case came to trial, she was ostracized by other co-workers and management. Several times she wondered whether she was doing the right thing, knowing that if she went ahead with her testimony she might be fired. "I talked about it with my husband and children. They all felt it was the right thing to do."

Shortly afterwards, her son stood up for a girl in the class who was being picked on. "I know that he was encouraged to stand up because of my example," said the mother. Both of them suffered from their courageous acts; the mother was fired from her job, and the son was targeted by other students. But both felt their sacrifices were worth the results. "My son learned a valuable lesson that will stay with him for a long time," said the mother.

Hopefully, all of us strive to be positive role models for our children (more on this topic in Step Seven). Doing so may empower our children to move from a passive role to an active role where cliques are involved. Even one child has the ability to make changes. Making sure your child knows that will give him the incentive he needs.

Things You Can Do

Learn whether or not your child is a bystander.
Give him strategies for helping targeted classmates.
Get to know your child's friends.
Intervene to stop malicious gossip.

Things You Cannot Do

Guarantee that your child will never be targeted.
Gain acceptance for your child among classmates.
Force your child to get involved.
Demand your child befriend a victim.

STEP SIX

Teach Your Child Tolerance

The climate of cruelty in our schools is based on intolerance for others. Children are singled out for their differences because those variations are viewed as weaknesses. But if we can teach our children to be open-minded, they will be less inclined to use cliques to torment others.

Remember the classic children's story "The Fox and the Hound?" The message of the tale was a simple one for children to grasp: Differences don't have to stand in the way of friendship. In fact, they can be the saving grace. The fox and the hound had fun playing together when they were small. Later, the outside world intruded, insisting that opposites can't be friends. The two found it challenging to continue their friendship, but they persevered. The value of that perseverance and loyalty paid off when the hound came to the fox's rescue, saving his life.

And so it happens with our children, too. They start out, in their innocence, accepting others, regardless of their differences or limitations. Soon, however, they begin to understand that not everyone is alike. Just looking around their classrooms, they can see the differences for themselves. Their classmates come in all sizes, shapes, and colors. Some are athletic, others maneuver through the day in wheelchairs or using crutches. They practice various religions and not all have English as their native language. While some children live in two-parent homes, others are being raised by a single mother or father, grandparents, or a gay couple. Students whose clothes sport the latest designer logos sit next to children whose wardrobes consist of worn hand-me-downs.

America's classrooms are a microcosm of our society. We are a diverse people and grow more so each day. What our children are now experiencing in school is just the beginning. As they move through college, into the workplace, enter relationships, and settle into neighborhoods, learning to accept and embrace the differences of others will be essential to their success.

Tolerance for others will also serve our children well during their time in middle school. In this chapter, we will:

- Explain the role intolerance plays in cliques.
- Deliver a wake-up call so that you can examine your own prejudices.

- Give you ways to teach your child to be accepting of other people's differences.
- Get to the root of prejudices—how our children learn to hate.

Warning: What follows may be painful for you to hear. We cannot teach our children to be magnanimous unless we are first honest about our own prejudices. Remember that middlers are quick to home in on our hypocrisies. If we preach acceptance while we practice rejection, the difference will be all too obvious.

Cliques—Birds of a Feather

In the movie *Grease*, the Pink Ladies attempted to change Sandy's squeaky-clean looks so that she would fit into their edgier group. Not much has changed since the 1950s, the decade in which the movie was set. Kids still flock to those whose attitude and appearance coincides with their own. Anything that makes someone stand out will not only make it difficult for that child to be accepted, but may also make the child the target of ridicule, even violence.

In order to understand the dynamics at work here, you have to go back to our earlier book, *The Roller-Coaster Years*, and review what we said about young adolescent development. Children from ages ten to fifteen are walking bundles of insecurity. They suffer from appearance anxiety, obsessing about their facial features, body parts, and clothes.

All middler insults—"That's so gay," being the major one—are about differences. Cliques are based on the safety of similarities. Those who are different are shunned.

When we tolerate others we respect their differences and allow them to be themselves, free of our criticism, disdain, or abuse. In middle school, with so many children attempting to hide their blemishes, there is little room for embracing the shortcomings of others. Posters hanging on classroom walls may proclaim, CELEBRATE DIFFERENCES! In actuality, CONCEAL DIFFERENCES! might better represent what happens.

Of course, many differences can't be hidden. A child's skin color, ethnic origin, disability, or economic status is often apparent to everyone. Our files are filled with magazine and newspaper articles and comments from parents and children who talk to us in person or on-line about the torment that greets those who refuse or are unable to adapt. Here's a sampling:

- Melissa Pages, then a senior at a Ft. Lauderdale, Florida, high school, revealed she was gay by flying a rainbow flag during a homecoming parade. People screamed, "Fags go home," threw things from the bleachers, and spit on her. "These were people that I had loved," she said, in the April 1999 issue of *Seventeen* magazine. "The school was my second home, and people were spitting on me." Rather than reprimand those who harassed Pages, the school's principal advised her to "lay low" about her homosexuality.

- In Amarillo, Texas, in 1999, athletes from the high school targeted the town's punks, who had spiked hair and pierced body parts. One jock hopped in his Cadillac and deliberately ran down a punk. He drove home with his stunned girlfriend sitting in the passenger seat. An Amarillo jury sentenced the hit-and-run murderer to probation. The defense attorneys had played on the public's disdain for the punk's anti-social image. The victim was seen not as a scared boy running from an oncoming car, but as a hostile enemy of the state of Texas. Prejudice prevailed. The dead boy's parents suffered two shocks—their son's death and the animosity from their conservative community.

- One mother came onto our site at "Parent Soup" to tell us, "My son is overweight and very self-conscious. The kids don't help. They ignore him. He has no friends. He has a fifty-minute bus ride in the morning and no one will sit with him or talk with him. He spends his entire day by himself. He feels anonymous. No one knows his name or cares what he thinks."

- After a talk we gave in a middle school, a sixth-grade girl approached us with this: "I'm teased every day because I'm adopted. How can I get them to stop? I'm not any different than the other kids."

- At a booksigning in Denver, Colorado, a mother asked us: "My daughter, twelve, has a physical disability. Her girlfriends used to be fine with it. Now that they are all interested in boys, I notice she is not being included in any of their movie plans or parties. She is so hurt. What can I do to help her?"

- One father intercepted his son's e-mail: "Kids from the outcast world join up for a reason, to make a statement. It's to show that even though we may have been rejected by some, we have not been rejected by everybody! If you can't be proud of being a jock or a brain or whatever, then you can be proud of being one of the outcasts!" Did his son's call to arms presage violence? How can we forget that the Columbine shooters viewed themselves as outcasts, too?

When parents such as the ones above ask us for advice, we give them ways to work with their children, helping them to reach out to others, to align themselves with those who are isolated, and perhaps to find a support group, if appropriate. Real change, however, won't occur until all parents recognize how intolerance harms all our children. There are many others out there eager to teach our children to hate. We need to step forward to teach our children to include others. The need is critical.

Examining Our Own Prejudices

Many children learn prejudice in their own homes, from their own parents. You probably would object to being labeled prejudiced. After all, at work you would never tell a joke or use a derogatory name against a particular ethnic group. Recently, you voiced outrage when you read that a local synagogue was desecrated. Are you intolerant of gays? How can you be when last month you donated money to combat AIDS?

Yet if you were to be perfectly honest with yourself, you would admit that your actions were motivated by other factors:

- You can't tell ethnic jokes at work because your office is racially diverse and to do so would mean career suicide (particularly because your immediate boss is a member of a minority group.)
- You were outraged that the synagogue was vandalized because you fear a crime wave will depress housing prices in your neighborhood.
- You gave to AIDS last month because your next door neighbor was collecting and you are making a concerted effort to win him over as a client.

If the truth be told, when you are alone with your family, you are never as politically correct as when you're out in the wide world. The other night at dinner you ranted on about your boss, calling him several of the names you never use at work. When your daughter asked if she could help out at a car wash to raise money to restore the synagogue, you told her, "You're not one of *them*. Let their kids do the work." And when your sister called to recommend a decorator, you told her you didn't want a "Tinkerbell" flitting around your house.

Perhaps you are not nearly so strident in voicing your opinions aloud. You may even preach equality to your children. But it's possible your actions are speaking louder than your words. Whenever you lock your car doors when driving through a certain part of town, or scurry away in fear and revulsion whenever a homeless person approaches, you are revealing your prejudices.

The purpose here is not to make you feel guilty but to show you how difficult it is to be free of prejudice. A 1999 study from the National Science Foundation and the National Institute of Mental Health suggested that 90% to 95% of us harbor unspoken prejudices. Uncovered were negative feelings in whites toward blacks, young toward old, Poles toward Germans, even Australians toward aboriginal people.

Embracing that truth is a necessary step towards becoming more tolerant. "Acknowledging the conflict between our values and our actions is extremely uncomfortable and is likely to be followed by a desire for change," said Sara Bullard in her book, *Teaching Tolerance: Raising Open-Minded Empathetic Children*. She added: "Tolerance is not an intellectual position. Being 'for' tolerance does not make us tolerant, any more than being 'for' humor makes us laugh. Tolerance has much less to do with our opinions than with what we feel and how we live."

How do we begin to put our opinions into action so that

we can instruct our children? We have to do more than just pay lip service to tolerance. We have to practice it with each and every person we meet. Here are some ways you can do that:

1. *Deal with individuals, not groups.* Most prejudice is directed at large groups rather than specific individuals. It's blacks vs. whites, Palestinians vs. Israelis, straights vs. gays, Christians vs. Jews, rich vs. poor. It is a lot harder to hate one-on-one. "Obsessive hatred usually finds its target in generalized groups of people rather than in specific individuals," said Bullard. "We find it easier to reject people in large groups, clearly distinguishable from us by some obvious physical characteristic such as skin color, than we do to reject specific individuals who are, we must admit, more like us than not."

You probably understand this theory based on your own experience. Do you know someone who is prejudiced against gays but is a big fan of Rupert Everett, Elton John, or k. d. lang? Perhaps you have heard an acquaintance make racist comments about blacks but this person still considers himself a big fan of Michael Jordan, Venus and Serena Williams, or Sammy Sosa. Is it possible to be anti-Semitic and enjoy movies by Steven Spielberg, music by George and Ira Gershwin, and clothes by Ralph Lauren?

Okay. These people are all celebrities and even the most prejudiced among us would still give our eyeteeth to share a lunch with Denzel Washington, Will Smith, or Oprah Winfrey. But this concept of dealing with people one-on-one is effective with non-celebrities, too. You may make disparaging comments about Asian "boat people," but fail to feel that hatred towards the charming Vietnamese family running a neighborhood restaurant. How about the Puerto Rican family whose father once risked life and limb to rescue your family cat from a backyard tree? And the Jewish woman down the street who has given so tirelessly of her time and resources to support the local museum has inspired you to do more volunteer work.

Contact leads to acceptance. In 1999, *Newsweek* magazine found that "up close and personal" has worked for gays. Two-thirds of the general public claim to have contact with people who are openly gay. As a result, fewer people now believe that homosexuality is a sin—46% in 2000, compared with 54% in 1998. A high percentage say that gays should have equality in employment (83%), housing (78%), and that gay spouses should get benefits from health insurance (58%) and Social Security (54%). A majority of gays (56%) say that straights are becoming more tolerant. Only 9% say that straights are less tolerant.

2. *Scrutinize group protests.* In 1999, a third-grade white teacher in Brooklyn read to her predominantly black class the book *Nappy Hair.* The book is about a black girl named Brenda with the "kinkiest, the nappiest, the fuzziest, the most screwed-up, squeezed-up, knotted-up, tangled-up, twisted-up" hair. One parent objected, calling the book racist, and soon assembled a whole coalition of parents who showed up at school to protest and threaten the teacher. Ironically, few of the parents had actually read the book and many didn't realize it had been written by a black woman.

In another incident in November 1999, conservative groups gave a knee-jerk reaction to a booklet produced by a coalition of medical, mental health, educational, and religious organizations which announced that there is "no support among health and mental health professional organizations" for the idea that homosexuality is abnormal or mentally unhealthy. Even though the coalition had stellar credentials, consisting of, amongst others, the American Academy of Pediatrics, the National Education Association, and the American Psychological Association, conservative groups called the booklet "propaganda."

It's often easier (and safer) to endorse the majority point of view rather than become a lone voice of dissent. However, the bystander factor, which we described in a previous chapter, also works with regards to adults. If you speak out against prejudice, you may find that you are joined by others who share your point of view.

3. *Recognize the destructive qualities of intolerance.* Racism can actually be physically harmful. Nancy Dorr, an assistant professor of psychology at Jamestown College in North Dakota, has said that the constant frustration inherent in being the victim of racism can actually increase blood pressure and put blacks at risk for heart disease and stroke. She conducted experiments where non-white and white men faced a debater who posed racist questions. Dorr found that the blood pressure rose more in the blacks during the debate.

In addition, despite gains made by African Americans, discrimination still takes its toll. Today, white people are born healthier and live longer, are more likely to complete college and have higher incomes, and are less likely to be crime victims than African Americans. The advantages of being white hit children at a very young age. One expert remarked: "Something is clearly wrong when young children, as soon as they get a look at the world we've made, are disappointed with the color of their skins."

4. *Dare to take a risk.* Being intolerant, falling back on old prejudices, is, for many of us, a comfortable thing. On the other hand, reaching out to others, challenging old opinions and attitudes, can shake up our world and the world of those around us. Unless we are willing to take risks, we will miss out on a golden opportunity to learn more about ourselves as we learn about our neighbors.

How do we take risks? It begins in small ways, like approaching someone at a party whom you might have shied away from previously. Volunteering at a homeless shelter or at a home for the elderly. Going to a lecture where prejudice and tolerance will be talked about. Reading about how various ethnic groups have evolved, what challenges they have faced, and how they have improved their quality of life.

This new approach may feel uncomfortable for us at first. We may even feel like hypocrites, trying to act in an open and accepting way while still feeling suspicious and wary. The exercise is like learning a new dance; at first we are clumsy and tentative and may even step on a few toes. We think about each and every motion, what we should do and how we should look while we are doing it. But with enough time and practice, the movements become graceful and automatic. We don't think about what we are doing. We just do it. Learning tolerance works in the same way.

5. *Treat your children with tolerance.* Children, particularly young adolescents, are often the targets of prejudice and intolerance, too. Think about the times you walk down the street, see an approaching group of young people and think, trouble, with a capital "T." Reflect on some of the things you say to your child, the way you treat him that conveys disrespect. Did you interrupt him while he was telling you about his day at school? Did you automatically blame him for tracking mud across the living room carpet without considering it might have been the plumber? Did you tell your daughter to turn down that awful music? Would you speak to an adult, one of your friends, in that manner?

In 1954, Harvard social psychologist Gordon Allport explored the roots of intolerance. He found that everyone has the potential to become tolerant. Whether we develop empathy for others depends, in large part, on how we are treated as children. You can tell your child to be tolerant of others and he may listen to you. He won't truly understand and practice tolerance, however, unless he himself is treated with love, acceptance, and empathy.

"Children who are brought up without strong bonds of family love, consistent discipline, and models of moral behavior become adults who are fearful, insecure, distrustful, and self-centered—the very traits intolerance thrives upon," says Bullard. She concludes: "Our relationship with our children can be the model for tolerance in our lives."

Nowhere is this acceptance more critical than with gay children. "Without the acceptance of their parents, gay children are left alone, to grow up in a society that reflects back at them utter scorn for their legitimate emotions" said Robb Forman Dew in *The Family Heart*, a book about her personal struggle to accept her son's homosexuality. What happens when a young adolescent who is gay is rejected by the family? Many run away or are kicked out of their homes. In a 1996 study of homeless youth in San Francisco, Hollywood, and New York, 10% identified themselves as gay or bisexual. Even worse, a 1997 study found that 46% of gay, lesbian, and bisexual students surveyed had attempted suicide in the last year.

6. *Learn to say "I'm wrong" and "I'm sorry."* Becoming more tolerant won't happen overnight. We may have to revisit the scenes of past mistakes. Do you have someone who, in the past, was the target of your prejudice or hatred? Is it possible to revisit that experience and make amends? You may not be able to actually apologize to the person who was wronged. You may, however, need to come to terms with what happened in your own mind before you can go on. Perhaps you once felt your actions were justified, but now applying a revised code of tolerance, you see things differently.

Even corporations are asking for forgiveness. In March, 2000, Aetna Inc., one of the state's largest companies, acknowledged that it had profited by issuing insurance policies on slaves in the 1850s. After reporting Aetna's apology, the *Hartford Courant* investigated its own activities and found that the newspaper had run advertisements for the sale of slaves in the eighteenth and nineteenth centuries. The newspaper ran a front page apology. Before the Civil War, many companies benefited from the slave trade and did so legally. But today, these activities seem reprehensible.

Going back is a necessary step for moving forward. In the future, letting people know that you are actively seeking to become more tolerant will help you to stay on track. This attitude calls for the highest level of self-confidence and courage, however. It isn't easy to invite others to critique your attitudes and behavior. If you can open yourself up to constructive criticism, however, the feedback could be tremendously useful.

7. *Learn to love yourself.* If you are a member of a minority group that has suffered from other people's prejudice, you may harbor feelings of self-hatred. Deal with your emotions so that you won't be passing down your rage and your own feelings of intolerance to your child. Join a support group if you can. For every person who discriminates against you, find two who are accepting. At the same time, fight intolerance in yourself. Just as you resist being judged by the color of your skin, your religion, or your ethnic background, don't judge others in the same way. As difficult as it may be, you need to have tolerance for those groups who are the source of your anguish. You should stand tall and proud because you may be the person who will change someone's mind about prejudice.

Bringing Tolerance Home

Our young adolescents are a willing audience for our lessons on accepting others. In a CNN poll released in November 1999, young people expressed great optimism about race relations, with the vast majority saying that race relations will improve in the future. You can capitalize on this youthful enthusiasm. Here are some ideas to get you started:

1. *Find the common bond.* No matter where we live, how we look, or who we are, human needs are the same. When your child talks about someone in his class being different, help him discover ways that they are alike.

Give him this example: One middle school class in the Midwest was concerned about a boy in the class who was suffering from cancer. When the boy's hair fell out after his chemotherapy treatments, the children didn't respond with ridicule. Instead, all the kids in the class, even a teacher, shaved their heads, too, in a show of support.

2. *Role-play with your child.* When he expresses intolerance towards someone who is different, ask how he would feel if he were in a similar position. How would he react if someone rejected him because he wore glasses or had to use crutches?

3. *Expose your child to people whose lives are different.* Visit a juvenile home, homeless shelter, soup kitchen, or retirement home. Exchange letters or e-mails with children who live in different cultures. Organizations like the Christian

Foundation for Children and Aging allow you to "adopt" a child or elderly person from another country who needs financial support. You and your child receive a history of the person and can write to him or her.

4. *Find ways your child can work or play with those who are different*. Is there a sports team in your town that is more racially diverse than those at your child's school? Could she take a dance course at the local Y where she would have the opportunity to be with children from various ethnic backgrounds? This approach works. In one extreme case, a group of Israeli and Palestinian teens spent a summer in the Maine woods. The camp was run by Seeds of Peace, an organization that brings young Israelis together with Palestinians and other Arab teenagers to build friendships and discuss ways to resolve conflict. After the young people returned to the Middle East, they worked together to film a documentary. The teens were held together by their common goal, to produce a good film. They worked out their differences peacefully, even when it came to showing how the historical conflict between the Palestinians and the Israelis began. "We got to know each other, for better or worse," said one teen.

5. *Watch what your child reads, listens to, and watches.* Unfortunately some of the media your child may come into contact with could foster feelings of intolerance. Television, in particular, often resorts to stereotypes when it characterizes various ethnic groups. Discuss this fact with your child. Not all Italian-Americans are members of the Mafia, and not all Chinese-Americans work in laundries or restaurants.

While terrorists in movies and TV are often portrayed as being from an Arabian country in the Middle East, there are many law-abiding Arabs in this country, too.

6. *Use the media to educate.* Not everything on TV is bad. Programs on specialty cable services like the History Channel can broaden our children's understanding of the world and the people in it. Each month, look through your television guide and select some programs which you could watch with your child. Follow up with suggested readings.

7. *Remember to stress feelings.* Your child will have more difficulty becoming empathetic if he can't identify and control his own feelings. Refer back to our chapter on emotions to help your child deal with this issue.

8. *Model kindness toward others.* Many of us who do kind works feel it is wrong to flaunt our good deeds. It's different with our children, however. They need to see us reaching out and being kind to others, whether that kindness is spontaneous, like helping an elderly person cross the street, or planned, like organizing a holiday party for underprivileged children. If you can, take your child along to help during these events.

9. *Encourage your child to speak out.* If your child is ever targeted for being different, make it clear that he has to speak up for himself. That doesn't mean fighting physically. It means fighting back with words and reason. Remember, part of the goal is to educate not only the bystanders but the clique leader, too. Say that your child was adopted and is being made fun of by a group of kids in his class. Here's how that conversation might unfold:

JESSIE: "Randy, you're so stupid. You don't even know your real parents."

RANDY: "Of course I do. I live with my real parents."

JESSIE: "They're not your real parents, the ones who gave you up."

RANDY: "The parents I live with are my real parents. My biological parents made an adoption plan so that I could live where I live now."

JESSIE: "Only jerks are adopted."

RANDY: "Really? Did you know that Superman was adopted? And Moses? You have an iMac, right?"

JESSIE: (nods)

RANDY: "Well, the founder of that company, Steven Jobs, was adopted. Do you think he's a jerk?"

JESSIE: (shrugs)

RANDY: "The next time, before you start making nasty comments about adoption, why don't you learn about it? Oh, by the way, I wouldn't say bad things about adoption if Tom Cruise and Nicole Kidman ever visit our school. You knew that their kids were adopted, right?"

By this time, Jessie has slunk away in embarrassment and Randy has won over the bystanders. If Randy had reacted to Jessie's comment with anger and insults he would have missed a golden opportunity to educate Jessie and turn the situation around. The bet is that no one will tease Randy about being adopted again.

10. *Encourage your child to speak out for others.* It's never

acceptable to remain silent while someone is being targeted for being different. Help your child understand his powerful role as a bystander willing to speak up. Give your child the words to help in various situations by role-playing with him. For example, one of Randy's friends may have spoken up for him against Jessie if Randy was too frightened.

11. *Humor is important.* Nothing can dissipate a tense situation like laughter. And because middlers are beginning to develop a sense of humor, teach your child how to use this tool to win others over.

A Journey of Self-Discovery

Remember our exercise in Step One where we suggested that you ask your child to diagram the school cafeteria? Chances are if you study the drawing, you will discover that many of the groups are formed along racial lines.

Beverly Daniel Tatum, a developmental psychologist, doesn't believe that these dividing lines are necessarily bad. In her book, "*Why Are All the Black Kids Sitting Together in the Cafeteria?*," she explains that beginning in middle school, young adolescents begin to ask the question: "Who am I?" They begin to think about their religious and political beliefs, gender roles, and educational and vocational goals. And for many, particularly those who are members of ethnic minorities, the search also involves finding a racial identity free of negative stereotypes. Young adolescents seek an environment where they feel comfortable to be themselves. Often that means gravitating towards friends who are from similar ethnic backgrounds.

Ethnic pride is more than just a catch phrase. For many of us it describes the deep feelings we have for our roots. Whether our ancestors came from Europe, Africa, Asia, South America, or were Native Americans, that heritage is an important part of our makeup. Those traditions influence what foods we eat, the religion we practice, the holidays we celebrate, perhaps even the language we speak.

There is a resurgence of ethnic pride these days. Sites on the Internet help people trace their roots. In major cities like New York, immigrant communities have established cultural centers and schools where children can learn about the history and culture of their parents and grandparents, and perhaps even study the language.

We all have a right to feel proud about our origins, and we should pass those feelings on to our children. There is a fine line, however, between pride and prejudice. Pride, even ethnic pride, can make us intolerant and suspicious of outsiders. It can make us defensive when we think we are being targeted because of our ethnic background.

When children seek out friends from similar ethnic backgrounds, these groups are safe havens in the stormy seas of middle school. A clique mentality inevitably develops, however, turning this discovery process into something ugly. Those who cross racial lines are singled out for ridicule. Blacks who try to maintain close friendships with whites are called "Oreos" by other black students. Similarly, whites who hang out with black students find their white friends have tagged them as "wiggers." Once our children hit adolescence, we can no longer dictate to them which group of friends they choose to join. We can, however, continue to stress tolerance for others. Otherwise, our children become easy targets for those eager to teach them to hate.

Hate Is Making a Comeback

There is a resurgence of intolerance afoot. A concerted campaign is being waged by hate groups to win over the minds and hearts of our children. What makes these groups so dangerous (and also so successful) is that they are using two vehicles our children love best—the Internet and rock music—to spread their gospel of hatred.

According to the Southern Poverty Law Center, the number of hate groups decreased 15%, from 537 groups in 1998 to 457 groups in 1999. Good news, right? Wrong! The activity among hate groups mirrored what was happening in corporate America. Smaller groups merged with larger ones, creating more powerful organizations. Many of these extreme groups forged ahead into cyberspace to enlist new recruits and spread the word. The number of hate sites online went from 254 in early 1999 to 305 in early 2000.

"The situation's very volatile," said Joe Roy, director of the Law Center's Intelligence Project. "Many of the isolated small groups have joined forces with much more serious players. There is strong evidence that far more people are now in really hard-line groups like the National Alliance and Hammerskin Nation."

According to the Law Center's report, most of the newer groups come from growth in the number of chapters of organizations like the Ku Klux Klan and churches belonging to the Christian Identity Movement. Christian Identity adherents consider whites to be the Bible's chosen people, Jews to be agents of Satan, and blacks and other minorities to be subhuman "mud people." The report, noting that twelve black separatist groups, including the Nation of Islam, now exist, remarked: "Hate is an equal opportunity employer."

Neo-Nazi National Alliance leader and founder of Resistance Records William Pierce is also the author of the race-war novel *The Turner Diaries*, credited as being the blueprint for the 1995 Oklahoma City bombing. Commenting on his group's phenomenal 1999 growth rate, twenty times the average for the preceding four years, Pierce said: "The whole climate for our revolution has shifted to more favorable conditions."

What does all this have to do with our children? In order for these extremist organizations to grow in numbers and influence, they need energetic and enthusiastic new members. Young adolescents, particularly those who feel alienated by cliques, make perfect targets.

Some of these groups are brazen about their efforts. This missive was posted on the website for the Ku Klux Klan: "The Klan is youth oriented. The young people of today will determine the kind of nation we will have tomorrow. Any movement that wants to make history must win the young. We are."

But those who oppose hate sites are fighting back. One organization, BiasHELP of Long Island, New York, snapped up a panoply of names that might be used for new sites—"swastikas," "klansmen," "crossburning," "whitesupremacist," "gaybasher," and "gaybashers." Anyone typing in one of those names with the ubiquitous dot-com on the end will instead be redirected to BiasHELP's website.

"The immense popularity of the Internet—particularly among adolescent males who coincidentally commit the vast majority of hate crimes today—presents a wonderful opportunity to promote tolerance and diversity," says BiasHELP-LI's president, Dr. Gail Barouh. "That means first limiting the potential for hate on the Internet."

Besides the Internet, hate groups are using rock music to lure young people. A good example of this marketing strategy is William Pierce's Resistance Records, the world's largest neo-Nazi music label. Pierce views the rock business as key in order to recruit young minds to his cause. "I don't care for the music myself," he admits, "but if it helps move people in the right direction, I'm all for it." The music, known as "hatecore," is gruff, loud, and guitar-driven. The lyrics, heavily influenced by the philosophy of the Third Reich, are anti-government and racist. The bands boast names such as Angry Aryans and Nordic Thunder.

"It sounds a bit far-fetched to adults," said Mark Potok of the Southern Poverty Law Center, "but rock could be hugely important in terms of enlarging the reach of the American neo-Nazi movement."

The frightening aspect of these recruitment efforts is

that these two vehicles are ones where parents often feel most shut out. Young people cruise the cyber-highway alone in their rooms or use headphones to listen to rock music. Unless we break through these barriers to connect with our children and let them know how we feel about prejudice, they may be won over by hate group propaganda.

Teaching tolerance isn't like teaching math. There are no formulas to memorize. Tolerance can't be taught in one semester or one school year. There is no graduation and no degree. Learning how to accept other people is a lifelong goal and, if we are perfectly honest with ourselves, we are all aspiring students.

We can serve as great teachers, guides, and examples for our children. When they see us working at becoming more tolerant, they will work harder, too. And that effort on all of our parts will open up our classrooms for everyone.

Things You Can Do

Serve as a good example by trying to be more tolerant.
Treat your child with love and respect.
Expose him to different cultures and experiences.
Help him find common ground with other children.
Discuss hate groups with your child.

Things You Cannot Do

Prevent others from discriminating against your child.
Change other people's viewpoints.
Make your child's differences go away.
Influence your child when your actions are contradictory.

STEP SEVEN

Lead by Example

You are a role model, the most influential one your child will ever have. How you treat your friends and relatives, the way you and your mate discipline your children, how you take a stand—your actions either add to your child's repertoire of social skills or endorse the bullying that earmarks cliques.

Being a model parent isn't simply about biting your tongue when you're on the telephone about to "dis" your mother-in-law. Your responsibility goes further. You must set examples that show your child how to be social and forgiving in healthy ways. Your life has to exemplify values of caring. We plan to show you how to:

- Model friendship in a positive light.
- Identify and remove antisocial formulas from your family life.
- Take an important stand: intervention.
- Test your parenting style on a pivotal issue.

This part of the book may bring you face to face with some mistakes you may be making either by commission or omission. As you work to assess, and perhaps improve, your life, you will be empowering your child. Furthermore, you are setting a profound example, namely that you are a work in progress. From time to time we all need to take stock of our lives and relationships, tinker a bit, and make adjustments.

Are You and Your Friends Cliquish?

You have a few good friends, but you don't consider your group a clique by any stretch of the imagination. You love a good gabfest, but that's not crossing the line into malicious gossip, or is it? Would you call this bunch a clique?

Melissa, Joan, and Patricia have known one another since their children entered elementary school. They became fast friends after joining their local Parents and Teachers Organization. Over the years they volunteered more and more, and in the end they became officers. Along with several other mothers, they virtually run the middle school.

Sometimes newcomers who attend meetings want to get more involved. As volunteer lists are passed around, a few write down their phone numbers. The three musketeers never call. The PTO board members tell each other that it's easier to organize the fund-raiser themselves, decide where to allocate money, or take care of the immediate business, than to explain all the details to strangers. That's a clique. The trio of movers and shakers are insiders who exclude. They don't want to share their power or inside information.

Or what about the following: The Petersons, Mary and Bill, are planning a big fiftieth wedding anniversary for Mary's parents. They're going all out. Mary contacted some cousins clear across the country and invited them to stay with her. She's decided not to invite any of Bill's extended family because she says, "They're not my kind of people." It's not the first time that she has pulled a snobbish act about Bill's sisters and her brothers-in-law. They may be less affluent and educated, but that's no excuse for Mary's calling them "coarse, trailer trash" behind her husband's back.

Mary's catty remarks are no different than those of a mean maven in the middle school. Without realizing it, many of us mirror what goes on in middle school. Keep these questions in mind if your middler gets wrapped up in a troubling clique and becomes defensive when you try to reason with her:

- Do you deliberately exclude perfectly innocent people from your inner circles? If so, find ways to be more inclusive.

- Do you talk about "standards" that qualify people to become your friends, those "standards" being looks, money, status, clout in the community, and such? If so, change your standards.
- If one of your friends tells you a secret, do you relish revealing it to others? Start to gauge how much conversation time you spend gossiping. Sort out what is hurtful.
- Do you get in the middle of family squabbles that become a phone chain of who-did-what-to-whom and who-said-what-about-whom? Or do you refuse to get involved in resolving these kinds of spats? Stand for harmony, not divisiveness.

It's time for you to give some serious thought to the way you behave when you are with your friends and your relatives. Improve yourself in the kindness and caring department. Concentrate on delivering positive messages about friendship. We've come up with a few lessons about recurring sore points among friends. If you model these, your child will be less likely to join or remain loyal to cliques.

Lesson #1: The friendship pinch. Maybe you don't even have a circle of friends. According to a disturbing trend, more of us are spending less time with friends. On March 3, 2000, *The Wall Street Journal* asked "Whatever Happened to Friendship?" Journalist Nancy Ann Jeffrey reported, "Blame it on longer hours, soaring business travel, and the flood of infotainment that keeps us wired to just about everything but other people. While countless companies have become family friendly—even letting workers bring pets to the office—friendship isn't on the radar screen." Friendship has become a casualty of our overstressed and hyper-linked age.

If you work, are your nights and weekends eaten up with supervising homework, attending school functions and sporting events? Factor in that old bugaboo, housework. It's no surprise that we hit middle age with the fewest friends compared to our younger selves, according to Jan Yager, Ph.D., author of *Friendshifts.*

You can't be a good social example if you don't have friends. Nor can you inspire a loner to reach out. Carve out time to rekindle your friendships. Talk about what trade-offs you need to make. Maybe you'll have to pass on that exercise class to meet your pal for dinner. Young adolescents think friendships just happen, like fate. They rarely realize it is they who are in charge of tending to such relationships. The message you want to impart is that friendship takes planning and continued effort.

Lesson #2: Shared history is precious. Remember skipping stones on the lake or walking along the railroad tracks? Who was with you? Those who shared your childhood hold a special place in your memory because they know the sights, the smells, and the feel of your own personal history. Some of us do keep in touch, even if it's only at high school reunions. Even if we don't, we probably wish we had. Introduce your middler to your childhood buddy by telling tales or locating old photographs. Even if you don't regularly socialize with this old friend, let your child know how lasting that buddy bond is.

Why is this so critical now? Middle school is a time of transition. Many middlers feel compelled to leave childhood friends behind. Your child feels he must choose: either to hang out in Tyler's room playing Nintendo like he always has or give Tyler up to join the cool crowd. He thinks he must block out those memories of playing *Ghostbusters* or *Ninja Turtles.* Show him that moving into new social territory doesn't mean he has to completely sever old ties. He can find time for yesterday's friend or let the union lie dormant for a while. Either way, teach him that shared history is a timeless bond, as timeless as the trees they climbed, the beaches they scoured for seashells, or the smiles they flashed from inside those superhero costumes.

Lesson #3: Friendship should be a two-way street. Next time you and a friend take in a movie or a sporting event, invite your young adolescent to go along with a companion of her own. Let the younger set watch as you talk about your mother-in-law's health problems or listen to your friend gripe about a coworker. Show your child the flip side to back stabbing. On the way home, when it's just you and your child, remark how good it feels to vent and know that a friend listens.

Ask your child if she gets equal time in her friendships. Can she reveal her worries and feel that her friend really listens? And cares? Both trust and a fair balance of power are missing in cliques. Explain that.

Lesson #4: Friends can successfully manage change. Your

best friend has a new baby. There goes your weeknight movie buddy, but now you know where to unload the boxed baby clothes clogging up the basement. Since his divorce your old friend is back in the dating scene. You get a promotion at work, moving you up and away from a coworker with whom you've become close. You lose thirty pounds while your jogging partner can't stay away from those Snickers. Being the one carrying the extra poundage, the baby, and not the extra salary can spawn jealousy. Where there is change, envy is close behind.

Your daughter's friend gets elected class president. A boy nabs a new girlfriend, maybe even the one your son had a secret crush on. Or, if your child feels betrayed by a jealous former best friend, help him separate the feeling from the friendship. "Consider where the jealousy is coming from—what in your friend's life is causing the jealous feelings—and understand that those jealous feelings say something about your *friend*, not about the *friendship*," advises Dr. Jan Yager. Help your daughter weigh carefully whether or not one bout of envy justifies judging a girl's entire character. Remind your child that no one, neither she nor you, is immune from an envy attack.

Brainstorm together about what options could temper the jealousy she feels or the insecurity her friend is feeling. Taking the time to work through this emotion is a life lesson whose value will extend well beyond middle school.

Lesson #5: Risk is a part of friendship. "If I talk to Danielle, then my new friends will be mad at me." "If I stick up for Gilbert, I might have to pay for it later on the school bus." As adults, we forget to tally repercussions from our child's perspective. Show your child when you are loyal to a friend and how you handle the downside.

Opening yourself up is risky because you become vulnerable. If you are a father, you are perfect for this conversation because males are wary of friendship. Feel free to admit to your child that you have more difficulty than Mom when it comes to revealing confidences.

Eric Mankowski, a Portland State University assistant professor and social psychologist, explains which standard barriers stand in the way for men. "Homophobia is the largest barrier. We're not used to labeling feelings of affection toward other men as anything other than sexual. Women are the ones who nurture and care about relationships."

Another roadblock Mankowski identified turned out to be isolation. Because men find intimacy more threatening than women, they keep their worries and their problems to themselves. As a gender they are less likely to share their insecure side, whether that means seeking out a therapist or sitting face to face and confiding in someone else. Men choose to suffer alone, bowing to a culture that doesn't allow them the same freedom it allows women to admit their shortcomings or insecurities. To do so is seen as weak and diminishing.

And finally, men didn't form bonds because they put little effort into pursuing companionship. Explain this male-bonding phobia to your son so he doesn't get caught up in denying himself opportunities for camaraderie. Explain it to your daughter, too, so she understands men better.

Expose your son to male rapport. Take your son on a boys-only fishing trip, or a round of golf. Make a mental note beforehand to talk with your fellow sportsmen about more than fishing lures or scores. You have to demonstrate the benefits of male companionship for your son. Sometimes being brave means sharing your weaknesses as well as your strengths with those you trust. Mothers and fathers need to explain the risks and benefits of friendship and bonding, and make the point that the rewards outweigh the perils.

Family Life . . . Not a Still-Life Tableau

Your home is your child's most profound classroom and your family relationships are a blueprint. The way your family members act toward one another, and how you discipline your children, each has a ripple effect. "Children relate to their peers based on the standards of their own relationship ideals. A child's ideal arises from the way his parents treat each other and him. A person carries this internal model of relating into all kinds of relationships that occur throughout life," according to psychotherapist Martha Heineman Pieper, Ph.D., and child psychiatrist William Pieper, M.D., co-authors of *Smart Love.*

At home, your child is absorbing social skills—or antisocial ones—and taking those out into the world. After talking with many family therapists, child psychologists, and teachers over the past several years, we've learned which patterns to watch out for:

1. *Is your household full of hostility?* Who among us hasn't gotten ticked off at a spouse in the last week? (We admit that we have). The husband who can't find anything, for example. Let's not leave out the wife who nags every time she opens her mouth. Modern married life has never been more stressful. We're all tired and edgy, including that middler of yours who's finally old enough to pitch in and rarely does so without an argument. There's conflict aplenty.

Are you divorced, a single parent, or a stepparent? There's ample grist for the hostility mill. Your ex is late with the child support or misses his visitation. After a long week you face the weekend dreading the silent or obnoxious treatment you will get from your stepchildren.

Hostility is a virus. It's contagious. If your child is living with mockery, contempt, and character assassination, he will bring it to school. A child steeped in a nasty soap opera looks distressed (the perfect victim). Or he lashes out (a bully-in-the-making). Both responses hurt a child because they turn peers away.

During an argument, never stoop to name-calling. Replace "You're such a slob!" with "When I come home to such a mess I feel stressed-out." Try to tackle issues by carving out time to talk quietly. Don't provoke a confrontation with an accusation, "Look at this credit card bill!" "Where's the child support check?" Resist the urge to push a spouse's (or ex-spouse's) hot button or to go for the jugular. Keep sarcasm to a minimum. If you retreat to separate corners during conflicts, you send a message that withdrawal works. What starts out as a cooling-off period drifts into unresolved stalemates. Agree to disagree, but resolve things. After conflicts, apologize. If you and/or your spouse or ex-spouse cannot control your anger, seek out a marriage counselor for a few sessions.

Conflict is always going to be part of our lives; that will never change. What counts is your reaction. Your moves either handicap your child or enrich her portfolio of skills.

2. *Do you ignore sibling squabbling?* Sibling rivalry S.O.S.'s come over the electronic highway to us all the time. "How can I stop my sons from killing each other?" "What can I do to dissuade my older daughter from destroying my younger child's self-esteem?"

If you fall back on what worked with younger children, namely staying out of the fray, it's time to intervene. Sibling warfare heats up during early adolescence. Middlers are supersensitive. Their bulging and blossoming (or not bulging and non-blossoming) bodies provide ample material for insults. They become stronger physically and less hardy emotionally. They become capable of delivering meaner blows. If you act as a hapless bystander, you sanction strong-arming tactics and verbal abuse. Your child will be more likely to take that sibling style of warfare to school. Draw the lines during family feuds: no violence, no cruel insults. Help your children identify the issues that are causing the tension. Let each child announce her gripes and grievances. Make each listen to the other. This forces a child to hear, really hear, the other person's side. Learning to see things from another person's point of view is a fundamental and pivotal social skill. Fair play at home carries over.

And by the way, if you are an adult sibling still feuding with a brother or sister, make an effort to heal the rift.

3. *Are you a bully when you discipline?* Are you (or is your spouse) the kind of authority figure who decrees, "This is my house, these are my rules, and anybody living under my roof has to obey me!"? Defining boundaries and setting consequences is extremely important. So is understanding and flexibility. You don't have to be intimidating, ruthless, or harsh.

Young adolescents are hit more frequently than younger children. According to *Clinical Child* and *Family Psychology Review*, half of twelve-year-olds are slapped, shaken, or spanked; the same applies to one in three fourteen-year-olds, and one in five sixteen-year-olds. A physically abused child is being groomed to bully.

Withholding your love is another destructive strategy. If you say, or imply, "Unless you behave the way I want, I'll leave you or stop loving you," you are hurling a dangerous blow to your child's sense of security and self-esteem. Girls are especially vulnerable to this type of coercion. A girl threatened like this is more likely to become the scapegoat of a clique or to rely on emotional blackmail to win friends and destroy enemies.

Children need unconditional love as well as discipline.

Families run better when young adolescents become part of the discipline process. In our book *Parenting 911*, we include a contract of rules and responsibilities for parents and teens to cosign. Make your child a partner, not an adversary.

4. *Are you negative?* Look hard at yourself. How often do you act negatively? Take note of how you label yourself and your moves through life. Do you say "I am a hopelessly bad housekeeper" or "I hate going to the office Christmas party"? If you are aware of your tendency towards not being positive, you can turn those assessments and expectations around.

Holding a negative view of the world is one of the recurring characteristics of unpopular children and bullies. These children think of the world as a dangerous and threatening place. They expect trouble and rejection. Like any self-fulfilling prophecy, this one delivers. The child gets the distress he anticipates.

Focus on change instead of shortcomings or fears. For example, if you feel incompetent at keeping your home organized and neat, spend an hour every other day straightening the house. This will improve your home and your self-image. Enlist the assistance of your spouse and children, too. By focusing on some positive aspect of the office party, such as linking up with an old associate or finding a mentor, you can look forward to it. Your failures are not personal reflections, only situations that need altering. Since children at this age are so worried about everything, a positive outlook is essential. When your child thinks she has a chance to make the competitive "mathletes" math team or start up a conversation with someone new, she is more likely to take the risk.

5. *Do you ignore problems or problem-solve?* Remember the toddler years? You were cautioned not to command, "Eat your vegetables;" but instead to ask: "Would you rather eat those peas or try a carrot?" Offering choices worked during those terrible twos and will work with middlers. Always turn to providing choices as a strategy.

Meet your problems head-on by fleshing out the possibilities. Engage your middler in the process. For example, you are asked to contribute a dish to a pasta night fundraiser at your child's school. After checking your calendar, you notice the timing is a disaster. It's either tax or deadline time, or you have a conference scheduled. You won't have the time or be in the mood that week to cook chicken parmesan. You could just say no. On the other hand, you could volunteer to donate a couple of dollars for the purchase of Italian cookies from the bakery or offer to donate napkins and paper tablecloths. You could ask your young adolescent to prepare something simple like garlic bread.

Problems crop up all the time—overbearing in-laws, a difficult co-worker. As they do, devise a menu of possible strategies. Equipped with this template, your child will not be stumped by a nasty encounter or a frightening social situation. He will tick off options and find something to try.

To Rescue or Not to Rescue: The Bystander Lesson

You've seen how you have to work on that bystander mentality with your child. When and how you take this stand sets an action-oriented model.

Standing up to a clique-leader or bully is a standard showdown. Behind every middler who butts heads, there is a parent. That parent is faced with a situation that requires a decision, too. Should you intervene and rescue your child? On the one side is the leonine reflex to protect your child. On the other side is the nagging worry: if I rescue my child he'll never develop the confidence he'll need to survive. Parents of boys tend to be even more confused than those of girls. With school violence on every parent's radar, the urge to jump in can be overwhelming.

How do you know when to intervene and when not to? You don't want to look like a cowardly or inept bystander. When you act, you need to do so with dignity and effectiveness. We have designed a framework to guide you if your child is being targeted. It includes dos and don'ts, when and how to take action, and when to hold off. One caveat: if your parent alarm bell sounds, listen.

Do disentangle your experience from your child's. Ask yourself: Are you fighting your child's battle or are you replaying a battle of your own? We listened to a Connecticut father who, as he told his tale, seemed to dwindle in size and revert to seventh grade, "A student was chosen to sing at an assembly, not me," he began. "I couldn't sing a lick. We all stood in line that day. I got yelled at for cutting up and saying something stupid about the chosen boy. My punishment was to sing by myself, instead, in front of the entire school. Terrified, I begged my parents to do something. They didn't. To this day I still begrudge them for not saving me. That painful performance is scorched on my brain! My parents should have fought for me!"

Clearly, the teacher here fit the bully category. After this confession, the father went on to say that he rescued his son anytime a problem ever cropped up. Over the years, he intervened repeatedly with teachers and peers. With the wisdom of hindsight he realized that his knee-jerk reactions hadn't helped his son. Make sure your past isn't clouding the present.

Don't assume that teachers are there to protect your child. You can't count on teachers. Why? Often they don't see the bullying because aggressive culprits plan it that way. Also, teachers sometimes think they are effective when they aren't. A Canadian study asked students how well their teachers addressed bullying. Only 35% of the students reported that teachers intervened successfully. The teachers were polled simultaneously. Interestingly, 85% of the teachers thought they consistently solved these conflicts.

Do intervene assertively when your child is physically assaulted. Your child has a right to feel safe during, and while traveling to and from school. If he is punched, pushed, or attacked, don't head for the bully or his parents. Instead go to the assistant principal's office and report the incident. He or she will probably be already familiar with the bully's history and family situation.

Keep your agenda action-oriented, not emotional. When a defenseless child is roughed up, a parent easily can become enraged or hysterical. Give yourself time to calm down. Respectfully remind the administrator that the school is responsible if and when harm comes to any child. Ask what specific actions he or she plans to take so that your child is not attacked again. Discuss with the administrator whether or not you should contact the local police. This lets the powers-that-be know you intend to bring in whomever it takes to keep your child from further injury. Filing charges is an option once your child has been hit, shoved, or sexually harassed. If your child objects, respond by saying that being assertive will get the problem stopped.

Do act on threats. If your child has been threatened but not physically harmed, you have a less black-and-white situation. Collect information about the child doing the intimidating from your son, any other peers, teachers, and school counselors. A verbal "I'm going to get you" threat, being stalked, or being intimidated via e-mail—all of these forms of harassment should be documented and reported to school authorities. Again, respectfully ask the administrator what strategies he or she plans to put an end to the situation before it escalates. If your child asks you for help, comply. It's rare for a middler to make this kind of plea, so take it seriously.

Don't dismiss the rumor mill. Rumors have enormous

potential for harm during early adolescence. A child who gets an undeserved reputation can end up depressed, anxious, and isolated. Whether gossip begins orally or over the Internet, get the facts and head for school. If you have proof in the form of notes or PC printouts, bring it along. Insist that the administrator put a stop to the smear campaign by warning the culprits. If you don't put a stop to slander when it starts, the next time the impact could be even more damaging and widespread.

Don't fight every battle. Standing up to a bully who assaults or threatens your child is appropriate, even mandatory. However, fighting every battle is not advisable. If you intervene too often, you deprive your child of learning to become assertive. Furthermore, you inadvertently increase your middler's odds for social duress.

Dr. Dan Olweus, Ph.D., psychologist, researcher, and pioneer in the field on bullies and victims, helped launch an anti-bully campaign in Norway after a rash of victims committed suicide. He discovered that overprotective parenting is a leading cause for a child's being targeted. Even when a parent is motivated by love and caring, a fix-it instinct conveys a self-defeating message ("you are incompetent") to a child. This subtle judgment becomes reflected in a child's wary posture and in the fearful emotional vibes he sends out. It sets into motion a pattern whereby a threatened child either tattles or becomes anxious and helpless on his own. A bully smells this weak prey a mile away.

Rather than intervene when your child is upset, the wise parent spends time working with a child to develop an arsenal to shrug off the emotional blows (options are covered under Step Four). In so doing, you are sending a message of confidence. Your child will feel capable of mastering the event, even if that means running from danger or spending time alone.

Parenting and Popularity

Were you popular in junior high school? Yes or no? That question probably makes you either flinch or smile. Either way, your experience with popularity affects how you advise your child. If you suffered through a lonely adolescence, you will be determined to help your child avoid a similar fate. If you basked in the glow of social status, naturally you want your child to have the same experience. But be wary. Well-meaning parents bent on improving a child's image can unwittingly sabotage it.

Do you offer suggestions on how your child can lose weight or dress a certain way to qualify for a more popular group? Popularity primers like that tend to single out a child's shortcomings. Have you found yourself saying "You are too shy"? "You don't try to get into the conversation enough"? Or even more confusing to a twelve-year-old, "You try too hard. Be more nonchalant (cool)"? Your observations may be correct, but what your child hears is that she is lacking something. Young adolescents are self-conscious to begin with, and so negative assessments make them feel worse.

If you are still smarting from what happened in your past, your residual resentment could bleed into your child's attitude. Do you eagerly agree when your child makes stereotypical remarks about preppy jerks or stuck-up cheerleaders? If so, your child will hold on to and harbor jealousy, and won't be open to different kinds of friendships. Conversely, if you endorse the popular crowd too heartily, your son will fear the reprisals of not going along with the crowd when they drink or use drugs.

Your role should not be to spearhead a popularity campaign. Instead, you need to balance your young adolescent's desire for social approval. Evaluate how important prestige and status symbols are in your life right now. A New York clinical psychologist, Louise Mini, warns, "Does your identity come from the outside, so that you need the right car and clothes?" If the answer is yes, it may be time to take a less materialistic approach to defining yourself. Are you bent on impressing relatives, friends, colleagues, and neighbors? Weigh honestly how important others' opinions of you are versus your own.

Here are other ways to put popularity in perspective for your child:

1. *Change your child's inner dialogue.* Your child is faced with the "*Am I popular?*" question every day. Take some of the pressure *off.* Substitute with a different set of questions. If your child is thinking, "Why don't the other children like me?" ask her, "What do you like about yourself?" Or "What do you like about your friends?"

Turn the conversation around at every opportunity to help your child notice her strengths and good points. The answer to the "Who am I?" question should be *more* than where your child ranks in a popularity poll. Talk up your child's achievements. "You really played your saxophone well in the concert. Did you enjoy it? Perhaps you'd like to find out if there is a community swing band you could join." Set up goals.

2. *Add a new set of adjectives.* Stop referring to your child with words that describe his social behavior. Cut out "shy," "unsociable," "awkward," "belligerent," "aggressive," "loner," etc. You get the gist. If you have a popular child, play down "charming," "attractive," and the like, too. Develop an entirely new set of identifiers. Give your child another way to define herself. Does she excel at learning languages, computers, fixing broken toys, building things, designing outfits, ferreting out the latest gossip about pop stars on the Internet, amassing a unique collection of something from matchbooks to Care Bears? Focus on her interests, passions, aptitudes, or talents. Then add these to your descriptions on a regular basis. My child is . . .

smart
energetic
musical
artistic
persevering
idealistic

curious
expressive
original
kind
[Add all of the qualities your child possesses to the list.]

In this way you are adding components to your child's self-image. You are giving her proof that she can use in her self-esteem calculations. If your child is a fashion maven, take her to a real fashion show where local designers showcase their latest styles, then get her a sketch pad. See if she is inclined to draw her own dream outfits. The middle school years are the years to expose your child to as many activities and interests as possible, so that she can get in touch with what she enjoys and is good at.

3. *Expand your middler's idea of weekend plans.* Broaden the social event calendar beyond dances, school elections, or sleep over parties. Having something to look forward to on the weekend will displace feeling badly for the child who is not on the popular group's social calendar, or it will give a child who is too focused on hanging out a distraction. Encourage your child to scan the newspaper for possible things to do. Get into the habit of doing this for yourself. Consider attending a sneak preview of a new film, a local performance of a musician, a workshop at the library on flower arranging, or a class on baby-sitting or CPR.

If she has an interest in anything, such as bugs, sharks, comic books, chess, kayaking, travel, a foreign language, or whatever, find regional activities or opportunities. Popularity doesn't determine or guarantee success later in life. Helping your child develop a passion or hone a skill does; these can be predictors of success and personal fulfillment.

4. *Test your parenting style on the popularity issue.* We've given you a variety of different ways to have a wholesome impact on your middler's social life. When all is said and done, the bottom line is that you are either an asset or a liability to your child. We want you to take a moment here to test your powers of comprehension.

Are You Helping (or Hurting) Your Young Adolescent in That Quest for Popularity?

The following test is part self-examination and part review. Take it to see if you recognize when you *are*, and when you *are not* acting in your child's best interests. If you are less of an advantage than you should be, you will learn how to become more of an asset.

Directions: Read each statement or question. Choose one answer. Place the corresponding letter in the space provided.

1. Your child is one of the few UNinvited guests to an upcoming party. Do you:

   (a) telephone the mother of the party giver on another matter hoping she might extend a last-minute invitation?

(b) decide to plan some excursion with your child to divert her attention so she doesn't dwell on being excluded?

(c) register your complaints about the cliquish party girl or boy and tell your child she's lucky not to be part of that crowd?

1.______

2. Your son insists on buying a T-shirt advertising a message or rock group that you find unacceptable, despite your "over-my dead body" objections. Now what? Do you:

(a) probe him to figure out what he is trying to express with this fashion statement and slip in your value-laden opinions?

(b) give in, after all, his friends are wearing this stuff and you don't want to make him appear too different?

(c) lose or damage the shirt in the next laundry cycle?

2.______

3. How would you describe your role in stocking your young adolescent's closet?

(a) You feel that it's your responsibility to set the limits on your child's style;

(b) You try to allow your child leeway to dress her way for better and for worse;

(c) You actively guide your child toward what looks best on her as well as what will make the most sophisticated impact.

3.______

4. Your middler is having a party and insists you *disappear.* How would you respond?

(a) You firmly insist you can't leave;

(b) You reluctantly agree to leave the house for a short while because your child is a good kid and pretty responsible and you trust him;

(c) Bristle, explaining that adolescents are accidents waiting to happen, and issue an ultimatum: either he back down on this or there will be no party at all.

4._____

5. Your child walks in the door after school with tearstained eyes. What kind of response would you give? Would you:

(a) feel you must get to the bottom of the situation even when he shuts down and refuses to explain?

(b) give your child breathing space—a few hours and some distance—to process what has happened to him?

(c) insist on knowing who is responsible for upsetting him so you can set the other child straight?

5._____

6. You hear from other mothers that a school dance is coming up. Your child hasn't said a word about it. You would:

(a) feel relieved because this is one less night of worry in your book;

(b) bring up the dance to see what, if anything, is holding your child back from going, and offer to teach your child how to dance, make small talk, or whatever;

(c) make a mental note that your child is hesitant about socializing and assume you live with a late bloomer.

6._____

7. Give us your most educated guess about your young adolescent's social status:

(a) As much as you hate to admit it, your child does not fit in and you are definitely resentful toward those who are responsible for this;

(b) You willingly admit that some of your child's social experiences are painful to him and to you, but you feel helpless to intervene and "fix" things;

(c) your child is popular enough, but you could make things even better if she would be open to your advice.

7._____

8. Basically you see the issue of school popularity as:

(a) a reality that needs to be put in perspective;

(b) a torture chamber that only a chosen few master;

(c) a brass ring that can be sweet icing on the young adolescent's cake.

8._____

9. Your child has a new best friend whom you definitely don't have a good feeling about. Your course of action would be:

(a) to keep your mouth shut meanwhile trying to understand whether or not your first impression is reliable or not;

(b) to trust your intuition and figure out how to discourage this friendship from blossoming any further;

(c) to befriend this child, too, so you can turn him around since all children deserve caring adults in their lives.

9._____

10. Do you think that clothes make the teenager?

(a) Yes, clothes count and teenagers often use fashion to broadcast their rebellion or alienation;

(b) No, at this age clothes are about fitting in and don't really reveal who a teenager is deep down inside;

(c) Yes, clothes are a potential and potent tool to win friends and influence people.

10._____

11. You overhear stories about harassment going on in school. What would you do?

(a) bring the issue up with your child and ask her to decide how she can make a difference;

(b) nothing, because this happens since children have always been, still are, and always will be, mean to one another;

(c) advise your child on how to avert the hurt and humiliation.

11._____

12\. Your child's best friend is starring in one of those making up/breaking up revolving door romances. Would you:

(a) initiate a discussion explaining what actions your child's friend should take to dominate the romantic script?

(b) heave a sigh of relief and thank your lucky stars that your child isn't in the grips of such a rocky romance?

(c) ask your child what he thinks—for example, why do you think your friend is so willing to be unhappy so much of the time?

12._____

Scoring Table: Fill in your answers in the spaces provided. Find the point value for each answer. Fill it in and add up your total.

1.	(a) 10	(b) 15	(c) 5	1. ____
2.	(a) 15	(b) 10	(c) 5	2. ____
3.	(a) 5	(b) 15	(c) 10	3. ____
4.	(a) 15	(b) 10	(c) 5	4. ____
5.	(a) 10	(b) 15	(c) 5	5. ____
6.	(a) 5	(b) 10	(c) 15	6. ____
7.	(a) 5	(b) 15	(c) 10	7. ____
8.	(a) 15	(b) 5	(c) 10	8. ____
9.	(a) 15	(b) 5	(c) 10	9. ____
10.	(a) 5	(b) 15	(c) 10	10. ____
11.	(a) 15	(b) 5	(c) 10	11. ____
12.	(a) 10	(b) 5	(c) 15	12. ____

Total Points ____

Evaluation: Find the category below that includes your total score.

0 to 55 Points. Too Negative. If you scored in this range, beware. In between the lines of your decisions and your opinions is a theme of outright negativity. Even when your intentions are good and your values in the right place, the way you operate is counterproductive. You see teenagers as agents of rebellion. You exhale with relief if your child passes on a school dance because where there are groups of young people, there's likely to be trouble. You expect your young adolescent's life to be marred by harassment and rejection, and are ever ready with revenge or regret. On the one hand, you are correct in that there are ups and downs during these roller-coaster years. But your anti-adolescent posture, depressing expectations, and strict ultimatums won't help the situations that face your child. Your son or daughter will, in all likelihood, turn you off rather than always hear the dark side. Negativity like yours doesn't help. It hurts you both. Most of all, your attitude prevents you from enjoying what's exciting about these years!

60 to 120 Points. Too Controlling. If you scored in this range, you see yourself occupying the position of ultimate influence in your child's social life. You want your child to have a good time, go to parties, look great—what's wrong with that? While your intentions are good, you want to play too overpowering a role. If you insist on knowing every detail so you can intervene, finagling invitations and making-over your child's clothing choices and friends, you are denying that child opportunities to make decisions and judgments for herself. And sometimes your efforts are bound to backfire. If you agree to become an off-site chaperone, however reluctantly, you are jeopardizing more than your child's popularity. At this age, behind-the-scenes maneuvering often makes things more unpleasant for a child. If you stay in the thick of things, sooner or later, your child will shut you out. You may always be right, but in the social jungle your young adolescent still benefits from experience. She needs your support, yes, but even more she needs the chance to make decisions—and maybe even mistakes.

125 to 180 Points. The Right Balance. If you scored in this range, congratulations! You are more often a sounding board for your child rather than the popularity Gestapo. You are realistic enough to understand that you cannot "fix" all your child's social dilemmas, her friends' issues, or her romances, and so you resist the urge to do so. If your child is left out, you try an alternative plan. Rather than jump into situations of distress with guns a-blazing, you take a deep breath and look to your child for cues. You make suggestions rather than counter-offensives and ultimately leave decisions in the hands of your child, even when that's hard. This is empowering for a child. You are patient whether your child is reluctant to go to a dance or too eager to latch onto a risky new companion. By not being overly negative or micro-managing, you deliver meaningful and positive messages: That your child is lovable regardless of social status. That she is capable of making decisions and even mistakes, all part of growing up.

At the close of this chapter we want you to remember this. As your child heads out the door on Friday night to join friends, or up to her room (closing the door behind her), it appears as if your parting words of wisdom are unheard or ignored. Given the choice between spending time with you or friends, friends usually win out. A young adolescent's number one anxiety and priority is: "What do my friends think?" and not: "What do my parents think?" And yet, during these years from ten to fifteen, believe it or not, *your* influence is never greater. Your child is watching you like a hawk.

Things You Can Do

Teach your child about the ups and downs of healthy friendships.

Work on reducing the conflicts that disrupt your family.

Intervene when your child needs you to fight off a bully.

Put popularity in perspective.

Things You Cannot Do

Evaluate friendships for your child.

Eliminate personal crises stemming from a divorce or a stepfamily.

Intervene every time you see your child hurting.

Make your child popular.

STEP EIGHT

Lobby for Change

It's up to us, *all* of us, to start the revolution against cliques. Fortunately, the issue of cruelty in our children's school isn't controversial like prayer in the classroom or condoms in high school. Cruel teasing and bullying isn't mired by church and state crossfire or opposing family values. Tormenting riles everyone involved. Taking a stand against peer harassment is a position with which every parent agrees.

The Search Institute, a nonprofit Minnesota-based "think tank" for adolescent issues, surveyed 100,000 adolescents in sixth through twelfth grades in 213 towns across America. After sifting through the attitudes, behaviors, motives, and needs of the sampling, they carved out a list of forty assets, building blocks, such as family support and parent communication. The more of these assets a child possessed, the greater her odds to avoid risky behavior, choose positive paths, and grow into a caring, competent, and responsible young adult. Do you know which two assets were most often *missing* in these adolescents' portfolios? A caring school climate, and the perception by the adolescents, themselves, that their community values its youth turned out to be the *least likely* traits young adolescents checked off to describe their experiences.

So let's get started. Remember the famous line from that baseball movie classic *Field of Dreams?* Kevin Costner murmurs, "If you build it, they will come." Say that to yourself right here and now: If I begin a movement to change my school climate from cruel to nurturing, parents will come and join it. Do it for your child.

Longtime trainers of aspiring grassroots organizers and co-authors of *Organizing for Social Change: A Manual for Activists in the 1990s*, Kim Bobo, Jackie Kendall, and Steve Max point out, "People join organizations that personally affect them. People join to stop oppression, prejudice, and discrimination that affect their lives. Such activities are often accompanied by the feeling that they are doing it for their children or grandchildren, which brings a kind of satisfaction beyond the issue of self."

In this chapter we are going to show you how to make your child's school a better place. We will:

- Alert you to a notorious turnoff that could sabotage your effort.
- Prime you with a 1–2–3 approach based on the expertise of professional lobbyists and activists.
- Expose you to a variety of possible programs.
- Get you started in the right direction before you close this book.

A One Woman (or Man) Crusade

When a child is the object of a smear campaign or comes home with a bloody nose, the instinctive reaction a parent has is to fight back. Even other parents who hear about incidents like these from their middlers want to take action. Taking episodes of cruelty personally is typical, and natural, too. Individual parents, in varying states of concern or outrage, call up the vice principal or the parents of misbehaving young adolescents and register these emotions. They demand action, apologies, or a guarantee that this kind of injustice won't happen in the future.

The truth is that neither an avenging parent nor a crusading one is particularly effective. This approach is too shortsighted. You could even go as far as saying this reaction is selfish because the effort revolves solely around the well-being of one child. And even if a parent *is* successful in defusing a situation for his own young adolescent, he is winning a battle against the culture of cruelty, but hardly winning the war. Parents must do more than address the indignities or injuries visited upon their own, or one, child.

Aren't we contradicting ourselves? Didn't we tell you in previous chapters that it is appropriate to fight for your children's rights? Yes, and that remains correct. There are times when you should call the principal and talk with other parents. However, you can't take on each and every infraction inflicted on your child, or ones that you hear about through the grapevine, especially in a climate of cruelty that starts around fourth grade and escalates well into high school. You have to imagine a larger vision for changing things.

It does seem logical that an outraged parent with a legitimate grievance would qualify as the most effective agent for change. Unfortunately, that's not how things work. A parent bent on avenging her victimized young adolescent doesn't cultivate backup. Rather than get behind such a guns a-blazing parent, others are inclined to get out of the way. And they caution their own children to stay away, too, lest they be wounded by the emotional shrapnel.

Acting so personally can and will sabotage your efforts. There is a better way.

Organizing by the Book

A school will never become a kinder or gentler place without both the administrators and the parent-teacher association getting involved. A parent needs these two powerful forces to turn things around. You can get their ears with a personal complaint, but you will not be able to sustain either one's attention with a vendetta. A principal will listen to you and order detention. A PTA president will commiserate with your personal tale of misery, but then she will move on to the official business on her plate.

A *me-against-the-world approach* at the principal's doorstep has dismal odds to effect improvement because it doesn't give others the opportunity to get involved. George Anderson, a well-known lobbyist for environmental causes and author of *How You Can Influence Congress* points out, "When people hear that Jane Jones is fighting for the Day Care Centers Bill, they'll smile and say, 'More power to her!' When they hear a citizens' committee has been organized to work for it, some will be moved to join and help. People like to be a part of something, and the existence of the organization gives them hope that something can be done about the issue. It helps dispel their feeling of powerlessness."

So instead of working alone and becoming frustrated, think of yourself as a lobbyist. Turning yourself into a savvy organizer will get others to join your cause. Follow these three steps:

1. *Recruit a few good allies.*

Do you see yourself as the only one speaking out about cliques? If so, you may have tunnel vision. There are many others out there whose children have suffered, too. Rather than focus on your child's tale of torture, look at a bigger picture. Cast your episode as yet another injustice, and as part of an ongoing issue that affects all of the children at your school. An issue-oriented approach appeals to the values of others and their experiences.

Ferret out allies and build a core group. Enlist the support of the parents of your child's friends. If your child is on a sports team, in scouts, or a ballet troupe, reach out to those adults, too.

Start with an open-ended exploratory conversation. Don't give orders such as "I'm writing a petition to outlaw cliques" or "I'm spearheading a campaign to remove a belligerent delinquent from school." Do say "I'm trying to find a few parents who, like me, want to do something to make our schools less cliquey and more friendly. Are you interested?" If a parent responds positively, immediately ask her for her thoughts or ideas. When others contribute their suggestions, they feel included, and more importantly, committed.

Next, turn to the parents of the children with whom your child or others have had difficulty. This may be tricky, especially if you have confronted such a parent about their child's wrongdoing. Cat fights between parents over whose child started an episode of scapegoating are legion. Come right out and say, "I'd like to wipe the slate clean between us." If you try to mend fences, you and this other parent can agree that all the children could benefit from an effort to create a more positive climate at school.

An excellent untapped source are mothers and fathers whose children are just entering middle school. Like their middler sons and daughters, they, too, are in transition, and eager to find new ways to fit in. Back in the elementary grades many were active. According to data from the U.S. Department of Education and the National Center for Education, three-quarters of American parents had high to moderate involvement in school when their children were eight to ten years old. As their children get older, however, involvement declines steadily. By the time children reached sixteen, only half of parents remained active in school affairs. This is because many well-meaning parents become confused about their appropriate role during middle school. Twelve-year-olds don't want their parents so close. Middle schools are less welcoming, too, as teachers have increased academic pressures. So this parent population new to the middle school experience is looking for an "in," and will be receptive.

2. *Build a coalition.*

Once you have a core group, widen your web. It's not enough to assume that others will join you out of the kindness of their hearts. While your agenda, of course, is to make your child's world a friendlier place, others in the community may agree with your ideals, but not volunteer. So take their agendas into account.

For instance, businesses always want new clients or customers. An adult might welcome an opportunity to acquire skills in, say, public relations. Single parents might be intrigued with the social potential of meeting a few new faces. Others may want to get to know administrators so they can send a daughter graduating from college to interview for a teaching position. As you go about building your coalition keep one question in mind: "What's in it for them?"

Contact your local parent group, most likely the Parents and Teachers Association (PTA). Your interest dovetails with their commitment. Attend a meeting. Volunteer to start up a committee dedicated to exploring ways to detoxify the clique and bully factor. Find one experienced PTA member to advise you. Having PTA affiliation brings many benefits. These experienced school insiders have contacts and know-how that will be extremely helpful.

Most middle schools have teaching teams. Unless you have older children, you are only familiar with the team who is teaching your child. PTA parents know many teachers, including those who have been supportive. Be aware that teachers, coaches, and mental health professionals have firsthand knowledge about the effects of peer problems on the student body. They aren't strangers to the young adolescents who bully or to the ones who are on the receiving end. Helping you combat harassment would make their workload lighter.

Look into your community for more recruits, too. Which clubs are active in your town? Boy Scouts, Girl Scouts, The Boys Club or Girls Club, area sports teams like Little League or soccer—talk to the leaders about your coalition. Invite them to join. Ask them how they envision their participation. That allows them to incorporate their own agendas into your goals. For example, coaches of intramural community teams may be dealing with more aggressive playing styles as athletes get older. They must weigh getting physical (playing dirty) against developing skills as athletes get stronger and more competitive. Opposing teams often are trained in unethical, unsportsmanlike tactics. Many would find a good sportsmanship element enticing.

Don't skip organizations like women's professional and business clubs, Rotary societies, religious groups, or any trade association from insurance adjusters or journalists. Most participate in community service projects. They often have a budget allocated, too. They may be happy to join forces with you when you make the advantages clear to them.

Contact the offices of local politicians. They are always interested in opportunities to enhance visibility and to expand their constituency. Emphasize your plan to publicize your activities. Approach local celebrities and experts, too. Like public servants, they need exposure. Star power, like political clout, attracts attention.

Your ideal coalition should contain people of many talents. Each person's skills will be valuable. Always assign tasks that coincide with someone's ability. For instance, don't ask an accountant to write a press release which she might find daunting. Do ask a natural writer, as he is more likely to say yes. Look to include these types:

- An artist: A creative craftsperson can design posters, buttons, and artwork to add visual punch to your effort.

- A financial mind: A fiscal-minded person can calculate the potential cost of your programs and oversee fund-raising.
- A writer: A wordsmith can create a slogan, turn out newsletter pieces about your effort, and put your program into a professional form to present to parent groups and school administrators.
- A publicist: A public relations expert can show others the publicity value in the program. Good PR is a wonderful incentive to everyone from students who want résumé items, to teachers who want good letters in their file, to administrators and superintendents who welcome positive feedback. It will also impress politicians and celebrities.
- A nurturer: A caring personality keeps a coalition running by making everyone feel appreciated for their hard work.
- A highly organized, time-conscious manager: A good manager will keep the effort focused, not rambling. The authors of *Organizing for Social Change* caution, "When you recruit new members, it is important to involve them in something in which they can feel useful. Organizations often try to build their recruitment around meetings. This is probably the least effective method for drawing people in, and if meetings are the only activity of your group, they may be a cause of dwindling membership."

3. *Gather Information and Pass It Along*

Rather than meetings, reel in your recruits by activating them with immediate assignments. Have them clip local newspaper stories about incidents of violence in your community or a surrounding locale; have them save magazine articles and identify local experts, too. Instruct them to submit any tales of clique scapegoating, bully episodes, or sexual harassment by e-mail or letter. Create a suggestion type box or affix an envelope in the school's office so that personal stories can be slipped in easily. Have them drop off catalogues, videotapes, websites, or curriculums that address these issues.

Every plan of action requires collecting data—analyzing the problem, comparing solutions, and researching possibilities. This list of questions will guide your coalition.

- What kinds of teasing and bullying occur most often?
- Are both genders involved?
- What percentage of the student population is affected? Don't forget to include the bystanders.
- What are the damaging effects of these misbehaviors on the victims, the perpetrators, and the silent majority?
- Is race an element?
- What about ethnic identity? Has one group emigrated to your community in large numbers?
- What kinds of solutions would change things?

Keep in mind that even the most enthusiastic parent, educator, or community leader is pressed for time. Ask your principal's permission to install a bulletin board in the school's office or vestibule. Announce your campaign to the wider world. Create a slogan. Join our "It's Cool to Be Kind" campaign. Provide a sign-up sheet for volunteers. Ask for telephone numbers and e-mail addresses.

Keep volunteers apprised of what you've accomplished. Have a committee member tack up brief summaries of what you are learning as you gather your details. Post the occasional meeting dates. Use e-mail, a telephone chain, and the school newsletter. And don't forget to delegate.

Choosing a Direction

Decide upon a specific plan of action. What follows is a smorgasbord of programs, a sampling of initiatives taken by educators, students, community leaders, and parents. We've categorized them for you. Some are costly, others free. Calculate which option suits your own school's population, needs, resources, and challenges. The descriptions are intended to serve as models or guidelines only. Feel free to adapt any to create an entirely unique approach.

CLIQUE-BUSTING PROGRAMS

We can recall a time when *Ghostbusters*, the movie, was all the rage among elementary school children. Our own children sang the "I ain't afraid of no ghosts" refrain while wielding weapons designed to annihilate giant marshmallow goblins. Little ghostbusters across America like ours have grown up, some into clique busters.

For example, Long Beach, California, junior high-aged girls founded **Circle of Friends.** Five hundred students signed on for the purpose of reaching out to other students, especially those who weren't part of the popular cliques. Each club member signed a pledge to make every student feel valued and important. They wore friendship bracelets to identify themselves and their new code of social ethics.

At Shenendehowa High School in Saratoga County, New York, students invented **The Respect Club.** The club had a faculty advisor and guidance from the local teachers' association, but the students were in charge. Members took an "I choose respect" pledge. They signed a card promising to tell an adult if they heard of any potential violence. An annual day was dedicated to publicizing this civil, dignified, and supportive way of treating one another. The club had an escort service made up of volunteers who accompanied a frightened or victimized student to class. Both social events and talent showcases were planned to spread the club's objectives of reducing discrimination and peer-to-peer harassment. Students and teachers judged outstanding in the respect department were nominated for awards. The club chose causes for community service, too.

If the idea of offering a type of friendship club appeals to you, make sure you develop it across social categories. In the early stages of organizing, include popular as well as alternative personality types. This ensures that the social club won't be misconstrued either as a dumping ground for losers or yet another perk for the popular group.

Clique-busting can be about geography, too. Certain schools created a refuge space within their walls, called **A Peace Place.** You've already seen how locations such as the cafeteria or the school bus are hot points. Counter these gauntlets and guillotines with a designated room, a comfort zone. This is a place where students go when they feel friendless, frightened, or distressed.

A Peace Place costs nothing. If your school is overcrowded, carve out an alcove at the end of a hall or in a room's corner. Many middle schools have garden spaces which adapt well when the weather permits. Enlist students to decorate the space. Adorn it with quotations that inspire kindness and caring. Have teachers rotate with supervision so an adult is always on hand in case a child needs more than just an emotional or social time-out.

BULLY-BUSTING PROGRAMS

In a workshop we gave at a New York State Middle School Association Convention, one teacher emphasized, "Don't forget to recruit the parents." His school district learned the hard way. They took steps within the school, bringing teachers, administrators, and students together to combat bullying. They ignored the parents. Their program failed because parents didn't back up the strategies that students were taught in school. If the same messages aren't launched by a triumvirate of parents, educators, and students, a program can't take hold.

A **Bully Prevention Program** is a proven payback of your time and resources. In 1996, The Center for the Study and Prevention of Violence at the University of Colorado (CSVP) analyzed 450 violence prevention programs nationwide in an attempt to identify the most effective ones. The tough questions asked of each program by the center were: Was the program design based on research? Did it *significantly* deter delinquency, drug use, and violence? Did the program work not just in one school, but did it shine in a number of different communities? Were its effects lasting? The Colorado judges rated Bully Prevention Programs a top-ten pick.

What goes into this organized bully-busting? An anonymous questionnaire filled out by students determines the scope of the problem and who is responsible. Teachers add their observations. In the classroom, bullying is discussed and empathy is encouraged. A school conference day is scheduled to highlight messages and skills, including how to be social and positive.

Teachers, administrators, or counselors intervene with known bullies, talking to those boys and girls and to their parents as well. Like the security company who hires former burglars to consult on safety measures, bully prevention programs recruit bullies, whose inside information helps them spot and make over other bullies.

Costs are minimal; about $200 for a questionnaire and

approximately $65 per teacher to cover classroom materials.

Sexual Harassment Policy Bullies are often, though not always, sexual harassers. These boys and girls can use sexually offensive language, disrespect, and intimidating behavior aimed toward the opposite sex or their own gender. Does your school have an official sexual harassment policy? Many schools do, but the policy is a lifeless effort, little more than administrative lip service, if it's not implemented. Activate your school's sexual harassment policy by seeing that these steps are taken:

- Administrators should clearly state sexual harassment policy, define what it is, and make clear what consequences will be suffered by violators. Posters placed prominently throughout the school get the point across well. Newsletters and school manuals should print the policy.
- Students must be told what steps they can take to lodge a complaint. An official form is helpful.
- Complaint managers, adults who are known to be fair-minded and approachable, should be appointed within the school to handle and evaluate charges.
- The entire school community, including teachers, administrators, coaches, counselors, nurses, parents, and students needs training on this issue to become more sensitive and knowledgeable. Hire speakers for

in-service teacher sessions. Plan programs for parents. Issues such as date rape, gay, lesbian, and bisexual rights, and gender equity should be included in student curriculum.

- Publicize the rights and the procedure so that those accused can be as informed as those making any accusations.
- For everyone's benefit, intervene and exact consequences promptly when a situation develops.

Since all bullying begins and ends with words, a campaign can be put into motion about **The Power of Words** in any school. In our presentations, we focus on language. In talks to students from fourth graders on up to high schoolers, we ask them to complete this sentence "You are so ______". We ask only that they volunteer those adjectives they hear most frequently. Ugly. Gay. Fat. Stupid. The insults shoot through every lively auditorium like crackling gunfire. Rarely does anyone shout out words of praise (beautiful, smart, kind) as forcefully and eagerly. Then we ask, "How do you feel when someone says those things about you or to you, about your friend or to your friend?" Silence always settles the crowd. The object of this exercise is to highlight the impact of the words our children hurl at one another. Our message is to emphasize that put-ups are much better for everyone than put-downs.

This good idea came to us, as so many do, from parents and educators. One mother's wisdom came from Arkansas.

This parent worked with her Southern Baptist Church Youth Group. They used a Put-Down/Put-Up lesson as a form of punishment. If a child insulted another, he had to apologize and deliver two compliments. He could not rely on superficial remarks ("You've got great hair"). He had to make meaningful observations ("You're a loyal friend" or "You always give 100% in anything you do.")

Surely you've heard that there's no such thing as an original idea. That's true. Richard Wendell Fogg, formerly a principal from a Washington, D.C., junior high school, recycled decades-old experience for his daughter's benefit. When he was employed as a principal, he heard students' shrieks of "fatso" and "sex machine." Along with his faculty, he spearheaded a program to recognize put-downs and rid the school of such language.

Students were sensitized to nastiness in movies, comics, TV talk shows, and sitcoms (this was a man ahead of his time, and before the rise of Howard Stern and Jerry Springer). He recounted for his students his experience as a young marine at basic training, and how his drill sergeant verbally demeaned him. His program was simple, really. When any student heard a put-down, he had to remind the one doing the insulting "We don't do that here." It worked. Years later when Mr. Fogg's daughter was in sixth grade in Baltimore, Maryland, he suggested the program to parents there. It worked again.

All it takes is the simple slogan "We don't do that here."

HATE-BUSTING PROGRAMS

Intolerance in the form of teasing, racism, sexism, and gay-bashing is a social disease. Curing this disease takes a social response. African-American Chuenee Sampson's story began the day a band of hate-filled white hoodlums pelted her school bus with eggs as it transported minority classmates through an Italian neighborhood in Brooklyn, New York. Along with a few others, Chuenee founded **Students Against Violence Everywhere** (SAVE) to fight back positively against peer, domestic, and random street violence. Young people qualify to be trained in conflict resolution and prevention. Then these peer leader/counselors visit other schools and spread the program's knowledge and goals.

In its first five years, SAVE established and expanded chapters in twenty-six schools. Our whole country could use more. According to the Justice Department, hate crimes are increasing, up 10% from 1995 to 1996. In 1997, President Bill Clinton recognized Sampson and SAVE at the first White House Conference on Hate Crimes.

Chances are, your elementary school has a DARE program (Drug Awareness Resistance Education), bringing police officers into school to talk to youngsters about how to resist the peer pressure to abuse cigarettes and drugs. You may not have heard of STARE, however. It's an extension founded by the Suffolk County Police Department in New York. The STARE letters stand for **Stop Anti-Semitism and Racism.** Police officers visit fourth-grade classrooms (now in 140 schools throughout the county) with the objective of making students aware of discrimination. They preside over role-playing episodes and dramatizations and have students journal how racism feels. Fourth grade is excellent timing for this discrimination-awareness training. It is during early adolescence when ten- to fifteen-year-olds first really digest the injustice and humiliation of racism. It is another huge stress placed upon the fragile shoulders of middlers of color.

GANG-BUSTING PROGRAMS

Statistics report that gangs are on the rise everywhere, not only in the inner cities but in small towns and suburbs, too. We've met parents and educators behind the numbers. A suburban social worker in New York said, "In our school young adolescents who wouldn't think of joining a gang *are* joining. With all the bullying, a gang looks like a good way to get protection." Of course, adults know gangs are far from safe because they go hand in hand with drug-dealing, criminal behavior, violent initiation rituals, and turf wars. Children don't know this.

As one parent put it: "I live in Illinois, St. Clair County. The rise in gangs in our town is just unbelievable. I do not believe these kids are the real 'bloods' and 'GDs,' but we have a lot of children wearing certain colors. Gang graffiti is scrawled on desks and on our stop signs. We've had several expulsions from school this year for guns. It's actually worse in our middle school than our high school. Even our little ones (and several of their friends) made up a gang name the other day, 'BOFB.' I asked them what this meant, and they told me 'Boys Out for Blood.' These are fourth-, fifth-, and sixth-graders!!! To them being in a gang is 'cool' because that's all the kids around here talk about. They make it seem like it's glamorous and everyone protects you!

"Our community added an anti-gang program called GREAT (Gang Resistance and Education Training). Run by the local sheriff's office, a deputy instructs a special curriculum. Children get DARE in sixth grade and then get GREAT in seventh grade. The children make a pledge to resist the pressure to join gangs. Let people know that no matter where you live, there are some children who have been exposed to gangs."

Another gang-busting program was the brainchild of an educator. An English teacher named Bob DeSena worried because gangs, divided along ethnic and racial lines, were well established in his school. He observed, "I saw tremendous hostility between African American and Italian students and nobody was doing anything about it." He decided to do something himself. DeSena scheduled a sit-down between the gangs. At the planned powwow, the adolescents realized they shared more in common than not. Coming from homes short on love and support, they all felt alone and needed the sense of family that gangs offer.

This meeting gave birth to **The Council of Unity,** transforming the gang members into reformers working *for* instead of *against* one another. The council sponsored social programs, after-school and weekend programs, and charity drives intended to bring together students of diverse cultures and backgrounds. It spread to schools throughout the area and into the Boys and Girls Clubs locally.

BYSTANDER-BUSTING PROGRAMS

Should you recruit your own child to work along with you? A simple yes or no answer doesn't apply here. It depends on your child. Some children may not have the temperament or inclination to be part of your revolution. Others may be very enthusiastic to participate, even take a leading role.

Here's one possibility. Is your child always listening to the problems of peers? There are boys and girls who engage in impromptu counseling. Their e-mail sizzles with confessions. Their telephones always ring. You hear them doling out advice. A nationwide program called **Natural Helpers** capitalizes on this personality type. The program, founded some twenty years ago, ferrets out those to whom others turn for help. After weekend training sessions, they become on-site mini-therapists. They learn how to mediate peer squabbles, recognize the signs of adolescent depression, and to be on the lookout for the danger signs for adolescent suicide.

If you have a child who lacks people skills, this next program will interest you. In Gilcrist Elementary School in Tallahassee, Florida, a service club called **The Red Ribbon Group** was set up by the guidance department. A mother whose son was steered to it e-mailed us,

"In fourth grade, my son's teacher noticed when playtime came, he sat and watched the others. So she invited him to join The Red Ribbon Club. Unbeknownst to the children, the club's agenda was to serve as a social skill-building organization for those who needed a boost. The club did several things around school such as publicizing the DARE program and helping others. My son loved the club and became more comfortable in social situations. It made his transition into middle school a smooth one especially in the area of his meeting others and making new friends. This club boosted self-esteem because The Red Ribboners did things that made them feel useful. They felt good about what they were doing and, consequently, about themselves."

Draft an Action Plan

As you've seen, there are a wide array of inspirational programs. We want to leave you with a few parting suggestions to attach to whatever strategy you use.

1. *Reach throughout your community.* In some towns, life revolves around the school. In others, the local church, mosque, or synagogue is the center of life for its congregation. Look around and join hands beyond race, religion, and ethnicity. The common thread is caring for youth.

2. *Add incentives.* It is hard to get parents to attend programs. This holds true everywhere. Give parents a reward for participating. In some communities this idea works: Since grades are an ongoing concern, let parents earn a bonus point on their child's academic record for turning

out. We support such a plan. Discuss this possibility with your administrators.

Another way to entice parents is to create a performance starring their own children. In Seaford, New York, the school district had difficulty getting parents to turn out for the substance abuse presentation. Discouraged but not defeated, they decided to enlist their student population and create a "show." Children were asked to write and perform skits and original songs. Themes and lyrics were on substance abuse, either how young people are tempted to try illegal substances or ways to combat those temptations. The mothers and fathers came to watch their children in action. In this creative way, they got the information the school intended. This idea can be easily adapted to illuminate the issue of cliques and bullies.

Teachers, too, are busy and not always eager to put in extra hours at programs. Appeal to the school administration so that they award teachers in-service credit for attending any workshops related to your objectives.

3. *Visit the local librarian.* Your library can be a resource center. Displays can be designed to publicize your program. Speakers, books, videotapes, and magazines can be made available to reinforce your message.

4. *Address intolerance.* Is racial tension brewing in your community? Are issues such as gay, lesbian, and bisexual rights on the agenda? Are gangs part of the community fabric? Talk to your local police who will be able to tell you what kinds of crimes are prevalent. They know if gang activity exists and how widespread it is.

5. *Ask teachers to include the theme of kindness in their curriculum.* Teachers dole out assignments all the time. Whether the course is English or global studies, ask them to probe themes of character versus injustice or heroes versus villains. Construct contests around the themes of caring and compassion. Essay or poetry contests could have contestants write about "What act of kindness made an impression on your life?" In art exhibits or poster competitions, artists could illustrate "What does kindness or friendship look like?"

And finally, invite the children to get involved somehow in your effort. Ask this question: What's your idea of the perfect school? We asked ours. "The perfect school is where everyone gets along," wistfully sighed a fifteen-year-old girl. A creative sixth-grader fantasized, "A place with no violence, no cliques, or bullies; that would be a perfect school where I can feel safe. It would have escalators, live concerts, and would not have homework or teachers who pick on students. It would be somewhere over the rainbow."

Now promise your child that you will make a concerted effort to bring that fantasy closer to reality. Shake on it. No—hug on it.

Things You Can Do

Be issue-oriented and open-minded.
Meld your agenda with those of others.
Find the program that focuses on your school's major problem.
Encourage everyone to work together.

Things You Cannot Do

Force others to take your concerns personally.
Override other people's agendas.
Fix all the problems in your school's community.
Do everything on your own.

Index